Outback

Lawrie Kavanagh was born in Rockhampton and grew up in country towns along the central Queensland coast. He joined the *Courier-Mail* in 1956 and has travelled the world covering sporting events including the Commonwealth and Olympic Games. A fulltime general columnist since 1986, Lawrie Kavanagh has published two bestselling books of his journalism, *Kavanagh on Queensland* and *Kavanagh on Queensland Again*. Selected columns from *Outback* were made runner-up in the 1992 Walkley Awards.

Hugh Sawrey, born in Forest Glen, Queensland, worked as a stockman in the outback for many years. On return from active service in World War II, he focused increasingly on his art, travelling around Australia painting murals on pub walls for his keep. Since then, he has exhibited nationally and internationally and his paintings are held in collections world-wide. The founder of the Stockman's Hall of Fame, Hugh Sawrey is now one of Australia's most famous artists, and was made Commander of the British Empire in 1988 for his services to art.

OUTBACK

Lawrie Kavanagh
Hugh Sawrey

University of Queensland Press

First published 1993 by University of Queensland Press
Box 42, St Lucia, Queensland 4067 Australia

© Lawrie Kavanagh, text 1993
© Hugh Sawrey, illustrations 1993

Typeset by University of Queensland Press
Printed in Australia by McPherson's Printing Group, Victoria

Distributed in the USA and Canada by
International Specialized Book Services, Inc.,
5804 N.E. Hassalo Street, Portland, Oregon 97213-3640

Cataloguing in Publication Data
National Library of Australia

Kavanagh, Lawrie, 1935-   .
    1. Kavanagh, Lawrie, 1935-   . Journeys — Queensland. 2. Sawrey,
    Hugh, 1923-   . Journeys — Queednsland — Description
    and travel. I. Sawrey, Hugh, 1923-   . I. Title.

919.4304

ISBN 0 7022 2559 2

Contents

Contents

Contents

Preface

It was back in 1963. The walls of the back bar of the long-gone Royal Hotel, opposite the GPO in Queen Street, were crammed with the works of artists seeking fame in the hotel's art competition.

Laurie Quinn, the publican, asked me what I thought of the mostly dreadful collection.

"That bloke over there has really captured the outback," I told Quinn, pointing to the painting of a lonely swagman shuffling through the dust towards the saddle of a distant mountain range.

"Yair! He's good," said Laurie. "You know, he's upstairs having a camp. Would you like to meet him?"

Five minutes later a wiry bloke in a stockman's hat, moleskins and laughing-sided boots swaggered into the bar.

"Gidday, mate!" he said, sticking out his right hand. "My name's Hugh Sawrey. You gunna have a beer?"

Laurie Kavanagh

I'd just come in from the back country ... into the Royal Hotel. The place was like a second home to me. Laurie Quinn offered me one of his balcony rooms to use as a study, a most amazing studio. From the balcony window

I could look out and see the time on the old GPO clock and the clatter of the first tram always advised me to get out of bed.

I began to paint all the facets of life I knew as a stockman. I wanted to show people in the city just what went on beyond the glow of Queen Street. In my paintings and drawings I have tried to be honest and factual above all things because Australia is an honest land.

When I depict the movement of cattle and sheep on the stock routes, every man is in his rightful place with the mob. When I paint a horse I paint a work horse, I don't try to paint a pretty spicture.

I have tried to show how the men and women of the bush cope with sometimes almost insurmountable circumstances.

In recent years, as Lawrie and I have journeyed to remote parts of Queensland (in the comfort of a four-wheel drive vehicle and not as I have done so many times by packhorse!), the same spirit of mateship emerges and I know that Lawrie, as he pens his columns on Aboriginal and white folk alike, really understands how the people of the bush live "beyond the glow of the city lights".

Hugh Sawrey.

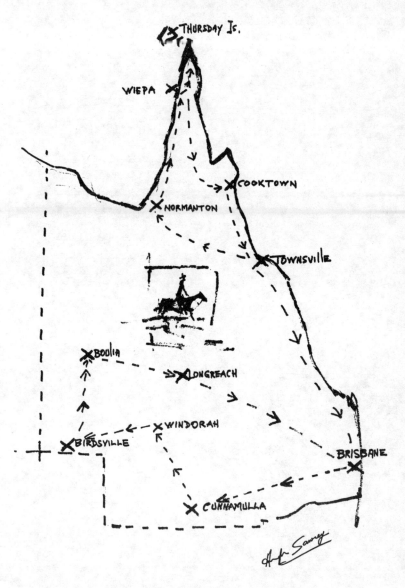

Hugh Sawrey's mud map of our travels

Channel Country

"YARNING A'WHILE"

SAWREY '92.

CUNNAMULLA

Ringers from Tilbooroo

Ultimately nothing stands in the way of progress and this is the way of the modern west. Time-honoured methods developed by our grandfathers, of stockmen and stockhorses, methods enshrined by poets like Banjo Paterson and artists like Hugh Sawrey, are doomed. Machines have replaced horses and men even on the most isolated cattle runs in the far southwest. Machines have shrunk vast distances, virtually wiping out the need for cattle camps and eliminating that cradle of Aussie bush story and song, yarning round the campfire.

Today the traditional stockman and stockhorse have all but disappeared and we're lucky to have the works of Paterson and Sawrey to recall those days. Mind you, they weren't always what they were cracked up to be, the good old droving days. Out west of Thargomindah a sick old drover told me he wouldn't go back to those days for love nor money.

"Why would I?" he asked with a hint of bitterness. "If we weren't wet and cold we were boiling under the sun. There was no let-up — seven days a week most of the time."

Sawrey has a different view of his younger days drifting through the Outback. They weren't all beer and skittles, he recalls, but great times just the same. There was no such thing as a forty-hour week and the boss never heard of overtime in the Outback. You worked until the job was done — rain, hail, or shine. Come Saturday it was "shoe-up" time, seeing to your horses and generally maintaining

3

your gear. I suggested that left Sunday for a bit of recreation. "Not blooming likely," said Hughie. "We were just too buggered to do anything. We might do a bit of washing then lay around camping for the rest of the day."

But they had personal freedom because the stockman's life was a nomadic one. They were drifters, mainly, men who rode on when the whim took them, and Sawrey did a lot of moving on from stations on the edge of the southwestern desert right up to the Gulf of Carpentaria. Why did they drift so much?

"I suppose most of the young blokes liked to keep moving. We didn't like to stay in the one place too long," Hughie said. "We'd be sitting round the campfire yarning after tea when someone would start telling stories about some station they'd worked a thousand miles away, and suddenly something he said would catch your imagination. It might be about the beauty of the country out there or the people. Someone might say it was a great place to work with a good boss and suddenly you wanted to see for yourself.

"So you'd pick up your cheque, go into town for a week or two to get the dust out of your throat, then throw your swag on the train and head off to see for yourself."

One of the stations Hugh worked on for longer than usual was Tilbooroo, north of Eulo, where he was head stockman, and he was in for a surprise from those long-gone days when I joined him in Cunnamulla at the start of our Channel Country trip. I was talking to Jim Wharton, regional councillor at the local Aboriginal Affairs office and mentioned I was on assignment with the artist Hugh Sawrey. "Not *the* Hughie Sawrey? Not my old boss from Tilbooroo?" Jim almost exploded.

"None other," said I.

Well one thing led to another and that night was reunion time for the ringers from Tilbooroo. Mouth organs appeared, including Hughie's, and it was nothing short of a rollicking great old-fashioned time in the Trappers Inn, a dusty Cunnamulla pub that hasn't quite caught up with the twentieth century, I'm happy to report.

There was, however, one discordant note that had been bothering Jim for more than thirty years, which he felt bound to disclose ere he and Hughie had downed their first toast to Tilbooroo days. Before they went their separate ways back then, Hughie gave the young ringer a memento of their time on Tilbooroo, an emu egg he'd carved by the campfire. There are several grades of colour to an emu egg's shell that can be exposed by gently carving the outer layers away with a pocket knife.

"It was a work of art," Jim recalled, rather sheepishly I thought for such a happy event. "It was a carving of a swaggie and was called 'Sunrise in the Jump-up Country', and I reckon it was the best present I ever received. I looked after it for years but one day a Kiwi shearer offered me ten quid and like a bloody fool I took it. I needed the money pretty bad at that stage. I'd give anything to get it back."

No chance of that these days, but you never know your luck when you're drinking over old Tilbooroo times in the Trappers Inn with a generous bloke like Sawrey. So before the night was over Sawrey whipped off his favourite Akubra, signed the brim with a message from the good old days, and gave it to Jim. Fair dinkum! One day they'll lock Sawrey up for giving his pants away.

Next morning I met Jim's daughter at Aboriginal Affairs headquarters and she said she'd never seen a happier man than her dad at breakfast.

"He reckoned we never believed him when he said he worked with Mr Sawrey on Tilbooroo, but now he's got proof that he's mates with the famous artist. And don't worry, he won't be selling this present."

Back in those days, long before Sawrey could afford the canvas, paints and brushes that are his tools today, the budding artist surfaced in many basic ways. He carved wooden figures out of gidyea, painted bush scenes on tobacco tins, and carved emu eggs and leather quartpot pouches with his pocket knife. He even tried his hand at making a fancy weather vane once and, talking to the new boss of Tilbooroo, Peter Tuite, recalled how he couldn't get it to swing in the wind despite fitting a ball-bearing race. He made the vane in the traditional rooster shape from a scrap of old trough iron, he told Tuite.

"It's probably somewhere around the homestead today," said Hugh. "I just pelted it out when it wouldn't work."

The boss's eyes took on a distant gaze and you could tell he was mentally sorting through the station dump, storerooms and sheds trying to remember where the hell he'd last seen that old iron rooster.

"You know," recalled Peter from what sounded like a fair distance, "I think I know where that old rooster is. I think I can lay my hands on it."

What's the betting that early Sawrey work, the battered old iron rooster, has been recovered by now and, dusted off, takes pride of place at Tilbooroo homestead, a tangible reminder of the Tilbooroo ringer who rose to fame — the Tilbooroo ringer whose talent for recording outback history on canvas is about all that remains of a vanishing Aussie tradition, the stockman and his true blue mate, the stockhorse.

"The Thargomindah Celebrations!"

THARGOMINDAH

London... Paris... Thargo?

Thargomindah may mark time in dry and dusty outback isolation today, but there was a time late last
century when it rubbed shoulders with the world's two
most glamorous cities as a global leader in the new age
of hydro-electricity. Certainly, when Thargomindah's
civic leaders hooked up its prized, high-pressure artesian
bore to a generating plant to give residents cheap power
in 1896, it was one of the first centres in the world to get
hydro-electricity. And when a proud local said recently
the order went London, Paris, Thargomindah, followed by
the rest of the world, Hugh Sawrey and I had no cause to
doubt him — because he weighed at least the equal of the
two of us combined and was twice as mean.

Dispute all of that if you like, but Thargomindah was
unique in Australia with its hydro power supply almost a
century ago. And remember Thargomindah had another
world first, thanks to the time goats ate the Methodist
Church during a severe drought because its canegrass
thatched walls were the only feed for miles.

The story of Thargomindah's early hydro-electricity
supply makes you wonder how residents of the day
viewed their town's potential. For despite its newness and
isolation, a decade after its gazettal as Bulloo Division
headquarters in 1880, Thargomindah boasted a population of 338 (thirteen more than today) and was serviced
by two banks, three hotels, four drapers, two newspapers,
and just about everything you would find in Brisbane,
including jewellers, brickmakers and hairdressers.

Thargomindah was the financial capital and trading centre for a vast, rich cattle industry. There was a solid future here, not like the boom gold towns on the coast which blazed for a mere moment in history. Thargomindah was rock solid. Why else would the governor of Queensland and his wife, Lord and Lady Lamington, make the 1200 kilometre journey by train and coach over devilish roads to such an outpost of empire at the turn of the century? It was on the threshold of something big, for sure.

Thargo's high society turned on a banquet fit for a king, not just a mere governor, judging by the photos spread before me today: gentlemen in three-piece dinner suits, gold watch chains and bow ties . . . waxed moustaches, of course; the ladies grandly gowned and coiffeured. And hats? Large, bold hats like bowls of salad, of fruit, of flowers. One amazing hat was topped by a bird about to take flight, several feathers of which appear to be poked up the left nostril and into the left eye of one unfortunate man standing behind the beauteous creature. Before them, a seven metre table under starched white table-cloth (with a patch discreetly hidden near the floor) bedecked with bottles of champagne and a feast fit for the vice-regal court.

Back in the late 1890s could the ordinary folk of Thargomindah have had any doubt that theirs was a metropolis destined to become a mighty inland city, maybe even a rival to that city of slothful ne'er-do-wells and ladies of the night, far-off Brisbane? They were awaiting the coming of the railway from Cunnamulla, which was already linked by rail to Brisbane. No more would they be forced to rely on goods carried by riverboats up the Darling and Murray systems, then by camel and bullock train through Bourke.

Little did they know that Thargomindah had just about reached its peak by the turn of the century and it was an ominous sign when the town's leading hotel, the Royal, site of the vice-regal banquet, closed down soon after Federation. Thargomindah remained much as Hugh remembered it from the Depression years when he passed through, tired, hungry and broke looking for work: a town of small houses with goat yards down the back and always the tinkling of goat bells.

"They kept goats for milk and they'd bowl 'em over for meat too," Hugh recalled. "A lot of people were raised on goat meat."

Today Thargomindah is a clean, pleasant and comparatively modern western town, but with thirteen fewer people than it had back in 1891, and a couple of thousand fewer goats. Hugh and I didn't stay long in town, just long enough to say gidday to Chris Smith, the publican, but we camped on the bank of the Bulloo River just outside, and did some fishing. Our spot was right next to the ruins of historic Thargomindah Station homestead, with its crumbling handmade brick and pisé walls and staunch wooden levee.

Thargomindah Station, the forerunner of the town, was established about 1865 by Vincent Dowling, who built the fine homestead a mite too close to the river. Dowling chose the site to please his young wife Fanny who loved the homestead's view of the Bulloo's broad reach. When you consider Fanny had left a refined life in Sydney to travel thousands of kilometres across a trackless land to live in the wilderness, choosing the site of her homestead would have been the least a new husband could have left up to his wife.

The station was later taken up, like so many others, by Sid Kidman, later Sir Sidney the Cattle King. Shortly before the First World War, a young Englishman named Gerald Gooch arrived in Adelaide to work for Kidman, a distant relative. It was the start of a long learning process for the new chum, as ringer, Birdsville Track drover, bookkeeper and station manager, before Gooch eventually bought Thargomindah Station in the early 1920s.

His daughter, Joan Gooch, well remembers her father's tales of droving the Birdsville Track. She heard them often within those crumbling homestead walls by which Hugh and I camped.

"It was a lovely homestead but became dangerous as the river channels changed over the years," Miss Gooch, seventy-one, recalled from her Bribie Island home. She should know. She lived all her early life in the pisé homestead. She would have been born there had her mother Constance not chosen to travel to Brisbane for the birth. That involved a 190 kilometre buggy ride to Quilpie and another 1000 kilometres by train to Brisbane. Mrs Gooch and her new daughter returned to Thargomindah Station after the birth and Miss Gooch lived there until the early fifties, by which time the changing Bulloo water course had made the old homestead too flood prone, despite the levee. A new homestead was built on a nearby ridge.

Miss Gooch, who is still in partnership in the station, remembers the last flood through the old homestead when her father rescued her piano by dinghy, storing it out of the pouring rain in a makeshift tent above flood level. Miss Gooch retains a great love for the station and visits it in winter months. Today it is run by her partner Ian Dicker and his wife Kathryn. Luckily for Hugh, Kathryn is a trained nurse and was able to patch him up and order, yes order, the artist to Thargomindah hospital when an arm injury became infected.

"Yes, yes," Miss Gooch said, when I started to tell her about the patching up and dressing down Hugh received from Kathryn in the homestead kitchen. "Yes, I heard all about it from Kathryn. But what I want to know is why didn't she get Mr Sawrey to paint a mural of the homestead wall with his free arm while she was patching up the other?"

As I said, Thargomindah may be marking time in outback isolation these days, but not so the outback sense of humour.

"SID KIDMAN ... CATTLE KING"

THARGOMINDAH

Saddle Days

Cattle King Sir Sidney Kidman probably never noticed a tall young dark bloke paying close attention during his infrequent visits to the outpost of his empire in the Channel Country about the time of the First World War. Why should he have?

Peter Hood, born at Thargomindah in 1912 and raised on Kidman's Norley Station where his mother was a housemaid, was just another ringer among hundreds of Murri ringers on Kidman properties across Australia. But the late Sir Sidney can thank Peter Hood and many, many stockmen like him for a lot of help along the way to establishing an empire that occupied 3.5 per cent of the Australian land mass, a staggering 250,000 square kilometres of Australia; enough land to carve into 400 million suburban home blocks.

There is no doubt that Kidman was a self-made man, as brilliant with cattle as he was astute with money and business; but in his time, from 1857 to 1935, expert help from Aboriginal stockmen came pretty cheap and plentiful. Hood, who worked on many far western stations on his way to becoming one of the most respected head stockmen in the area, reckons the pastoral industry may have not reached the heights it did without the help of Aboriginal stockmen, and no one with cattle country experience will doubt him.

"Murris are naturals with horses and cattle," Hood told me in Cunnamulla. "They are born and bred for riding horses and it's sad to see their jobs working cattle taken over by aeroplanes and motor bikes."

At eighty years of age Peter Hood was out of the industry before aerial and motorbike mustering had made the impact it has today. He was an integral part of the stockhorse era, his whole working life spent in the saddle seven days a week, almost twelve months a year, taking orders in his younger days, but giving them when he became head stockman soon after the war. His wages ranged from two bob a week soon after the First World War up to a couple of quid after the Second World War; that was plus tucker and what he remembers as pretty good housing. He was the valued head stockman on Nockatunga Station, west of Thargomindah, which is today owned by Kerry Packer. His wide-ranging working life and his skill as a horseman have made Peter Hood something of a folk hero in many far-flung places in the west.

From all accounts of people I met along the 3300 kilometres of back tracks Hugh and I drove from Cunnamulla to Longreach, Hood was one of the top stockmen of his age. According to a Longreach woman, had Peter Hood been born white he would have been recognised as one of the best polo players in the west. As it was, he captained the Bundoora Polo Club which won the Corones Cup, one of the major polo trophies in the far west.

Out around Nockatunga they reckoned he was the best stockman that side of the Gulf. A Hervey Bay resident, former government seismic driller Bob Larter, recalled an exciting day in his life from the sixties, when he and his workmates were camped at beautiful Noccundra Waterhole on Nockatunga. Early one Sunday the station manager unexpectedly roused them out of their swags. Some of his men had got on the booze in Thargomindah and not made it back for urgent bronco branding; hard-yakka branding, in an open yard where the cattle must be roped and snigged up to a bronco ramp for leg-roping, throwing and branding.

Larter had some experience in conventional crush-method branding in established cattle yards so he was put in charge of the branding fire and irons, all the while keeping one eye on the wild desert cattle that were running mad and loose around him. But he needn't have worried, he said, because he was told later he was under the watchful eye of the head stockman, Peter Hood, all the while ready to step in at the first sign of trouble.

"The best stockman in the west was looking after me, they told me later," Larter said.

Hood has total recall of his early days and well remembers Sir Sidney Kidman's occasional visits to Norley and other Kidman stations he worked on earlier this century.

"There weren't any motor cars then, in fact I was twenty-three years before I saw my first car," Hood said. "Old Kidman used to arrive in a flash buggy all the way from Adelaide. He used to come up through Bourke, same way as we got our stores and tucker on the camel trains from Adelaide. He was always dressed up in a suit and tie and he had a fine goatee beard."

Aboriginal workers on the station were glad to see Kidman around Christmas because it meant presents for all. "Each Christmas the old fella gave all Aboriginal workers new pants and shirts, boots, hat and a pocket knife. And the women didn't miss out. They'd get new dresses, good ones too, and stockings, not just socks — real stockings! We used to look forward to those visits."

Little wonder when Aboriginal stockmen were being paid about two shillings a week earlier this century.

"I reckon I might have been better off with the couple of bob a week we got in those days. Two bob meant something back then. We really appreciated it. When I was working on Norley and the big two-day Thargomindah race meeting came long, they'd give us two bob on the first day and we'd ride eighteen miles to town. Next day back at Norley they'd give us another two bob and we'd ride to town again for the last day's races."

Kidman was known as a tough but fair man with all his workers, black and white. There is a story about him sacking a white stockman on the spot for wasting a wax match to light his pipe when he could have used a stick from the campfire. The worker protested that they were his matches and he could do what he liked with them. Kidman told him if he had no respect for saving his own property then he certainly wouldn't have any for others' property. The stockman picked up his cheque and rode on.

Kidman was thirteen years old with just five bob in his pocket when he left his Adelaide home on a one-eyed horse named Cyclops. He didn't get to own 3.5 per cent of Australia by wasting money or making poor investments. There was one investment, however, he must have regretted for the rest of his life. It was in the early days of BHP when he exchanged cattle worth $60 for a one-fourteenth share in the fledgling mining company. Soon after he saw a quick profit and sold the share for $100. On 1992 value those shares would be worth $1.617 billion.

But such mistakes are minor setbacks for men like Kidman who know how to take care of their pennies. He often saved money on rail freight for urgently needed goods on outlying stations by sending them as "luggage" with an employee, a former jockey, dressed in short pants and travelling on a child's fare. With methods like that, and with an unlimited team of first class stockmen like Peter Hood at his disposal, is it little wonder that Sidney Kidman became the biggest landholder Australia is likely to see?

GIBBER COUNTRY

NOCKATUNGA STATION

One Gibber Plain
After Another

We were almost 2000 kilometres west of Brisbane, Sawrey and me, standing at dusk by a bold red sandhill on the fringe of the Simpson Desert. That day we had driven for hours over a featureless landscape with nothing to smudge or crinkle a 360 degree panorama of the dead flat rim of the world. It was as if Destiny had described the dividing line between earth and sky with a very straight ruler and a very, very steady hand. All day we had seen no surface water and little movement other than scant bird life as we drove a couple of hundred kilometres towards the western desert far north of Birdsville. We had enough water, fuel, food and radio communication to cover almost any emergency, yet we just could not escape the towering menace of that vast, dry timeless land in the centre of Australia.

So what made them do it? I asked Hugh for the tenth time that day. What made explorers like Leichhardt, Landsborough, Sturt, Burke and Wills walk off into this unknown, this void, in some cases to a slow and lonely death? More to the point what made them keep going when, doubtlessly bone weary, they trudged across one parched gibber plain only to face another . . . climbed one giant red sandhill only to see hundreds more marching in from the horizon like a loathed enemy?

There were rewards of glory for the successful but no second chances for the losers and, in some cases, the losers even got a kick in the teeth in death. Poor ill-fated

Robert Burke was criticised for not taking the saddle off his favourite horse before he put it out of its misery with a single shot shortly before he too perished. Can you imagine that? I've often wondered what made men go off into the unknown like those explorers of a century and a half ago but now, having experienced the utter isolation and harshness of Queensland's far southwest corner, I'm convinced I'll go to my grave ignorant. There is no logical explanation.

Still, their successes and failures opened the centre of Australia and fascinated the world much as man's first footprints on the moon fascinated my generation all those years later. The disappearance of Ludwig Leichhardt and his expedition out there in 1848 became a major mystery in Europe as well as Australia and sparked many theories and many searches which led to more lonely deaths. Years later more search parties tracked into the desert looking for a wild white man reported living with Aborigines and thought to be Adolf Classon, Leichhardt's second in command.

Even today men search for the remains of the Leichhardt searchers, men like South Australian Mark Prance, an oilfield production supervisor with Santos who has worked for years around the Queensland, New South Wales and South Australian border area. Hugh and I met Prance in the Noccundra Hotel, 130 kilometres west of Thargomindah on Nockatunga Station, which figured prominently in one tragic Leichhardt search. Prance spends much of his spare time in the desert looking for the grave of the leader of the Leichhardt search party which left Nockatunga Station in 1874, a rogue bushman named Andrew Hume.

To say Hume led a most unusual search party from Nockatunga is an understatement. Former Flying Doctor, Les Perrin, has turned the story into a fine book, *The Mystery of the Leichhardt Survivor*. Briefly, Hume, who had served time for a drunken robbery under arms, had been deserted by his original search party soon after it left Sydney on the long ride to Nockatunga. Flood rains disorganised the party from the outset, but Hume made matters worse when he hit the booze at every shanty along the way. North of Maitland the rest of the party cleared out.

Amazingly Hume was soon joined by a British Rifle Brigade hero, Irishman Timothy O'Hea, who had won the Victoria Cross in Canada in 1866 and had just arrived in Australia. Hume and O'Hea were later joined by Lewis Thompson, an experienced bushman and part-time piano tuner. I did mention this was a most unusual search party; a boozing ex-convict, an Irish Victoria Cross winner and a part-time piano tuner . . .

The party's final chapter centred on Hume's overconfidence in his ability to find water after leaving Nockatunga. He and O'Hea perished but Thompson made it back to the station and led a rescue party to Hume's body. O'Hea was never found and this in turn led to more stories of another white man living with Aborigines. Even as late as 1960 residents at Nockatunga remembered an old Aboriginal woman recalling a white man living with her tribe late last century. Hume's body was buried where it lay but the years have wiped its location from modern memory.

Today Mark Prance drives over the gibber plains and the red sandhills looking for Hume's grave and maybe, with a little luck, the bones of an Irish hero. They are out there, bleached and worn by the sun and sand, somewhere west of the Noccundra pub, and Prance is pretty determined to find them. So too is Sawrey. When he heard Prance tell the story of his search for the Leichhardt searchers he offered to give him a hand.

They offered me a place in the expedition but, having seen the country in that far southwest corner, I'm not so sure. Remember I'm the one who will never understand what drives men into the unknown with not a clue what might lie over the next sandhill. I'm pretty content knowing where my next stubby's coming from, see. I don't know how I'd handle it. Would I turn out like the notorious Melbourne socialite, Dr James Murray, second in command of Duncan McIntyre's Leichhardt search party in 1866?

McIntyre's party was government backed and well prepared for any event, but was still forced to turn back after finding the Cooper dry. As leader, McIntyre made a gallant dash back to their last waterhole where he loaded water on to a couple of camels and made it back to save the rest of the party. He was hardly out of sight on this mercy dash when Dr Murray slashed open some bags of flour to reveal a good supply of brandy he'd stashed there earlier. Incredible as it sounds today, all but two of an expedition which was in deadly peril got falling-down drunk in the wilderness. Sixty fully laden packhorses, left unattended during the drunken binge, wandered off into the desert to die.

McIntyre returned with the lifesaving water to find his men legless and most of his stores gone. He sacked Dr Murray and several others on the spot but even that was a mistake because Murray returned to Melbourne with his version of the near disaster, naturally with himself as the hero.

Eventually Dr Murray was discredited; he turned to black-birding and was generally held responsible for the slaughter of 70 Polynesians locked up in the hold of his ship. He escaped the gallows by turning Queen's evidence, but a letter to the editor of the *Sydney Morning Herald* in 1873 summed up the mad doctor pretty well. Signed by his father, the letter stated that Dr Murray had been cut off from his family "as a disgrace to creed, country and family" and should be the first to be hung for the slaughter.

See what happens to people who venture too far into Queensland's southwest in search of lost expeditions? You wouldn't want that to happen to me too, would you? Huh?

SAWREY '91

HADDON CORNER

Bucking Mickeys

The flies were something awful in the Channel Country this summer — the worst plague of blinking flies in almost twenty years, one old bloke said. We didn't need to be told though, and for the first time in my life I pulled on a fly veil, a nylon model that was hot as blazes. Mark Prance, the oilfield supervisor we met in the Noccundra pub, gave Hugh and me a couple and while I reckon it was better than nothing, Hugh got mad as hell with his, ripped out his pocket knife and made a few alterations that resulted in a small pile of cut-up mosquito net and a face full of flies.

Hugh doesn't whinge much but he couldn't stop complaining they didn't make fly veils like they used to when he was chasing wild cattle out there about half a century ago. The mesh should be big enough to let the floody flies out once they get in, he kept saying. But we didn't see any of those old-fashioned nets until right near the end of our trip at Winton.

That's how come Hugh looked a pretty strange sight weeks earlier when three strangers approached our camp on a waterhole just east of Betoota. He was wearing an onion bag over his head, an orange-coloured onion bag, as he squatted by the campfire cooking some small jewfish for breakfast. I reckon locals don't often see travellers wearing orange-coloured onion bags over their heads at breakfast time, so you can imagine these blokes approached our camp with caution. But they were polite enough not to mention the onion bag even when they introduced themselves as Simon Daley, Toby Gorringe and Cameron Steffan from Mt Leonard Station, just down the track a bit. I was half expecting a blast for poaching their bloody fish or lighting an unauthorised fire or illegal camping or something, but all they wanted was to offer us the men's quarters at the homestead away from the bloody flies. It wasn't a hard decision and we decided to break camp as soon as possible and meet them later near a bronco yard at Haddon Corner — that's out where the Queensland-South Australian border stops running west to east and plunges south to New South Wales. It's a good place to go if you want a little peace and quiet. But for heck's sake listen to directions before you take off. I leave all that to Hughie because he understands when country people talk about gidyea trees, clumps of spinifex and jump-ups as if they were prominent street signs.

After crossing miles of gibber plains and dry creeks and making correct decisions at a dozen or more forks in the track, we spotted Simon on his haunches, sensibly clutching a waterbag by the road, waiting to lead us further into the unknown. The country out that way isn't exactly spectacular in a grand sense but it's breathtaking in its arid vastness and you could tell Hugh's spirits were lifting the further we drove into it because it reminded him of his days out there as a young stockman, particularly around the bronco yards.

Now, if you haven't been out where the stations are measured in thousands not hundreds of square kilometres, you may never have heard the term "broncoing". Sure, we've all heard the Yank term "bronco" for horse — of Spanish origin, I believe. And because of its American connotations some of us were dirty when the Brisbane Rugby League team adopted the name. But the act of "broncoing" is as Aussie as you can get and has been synonymous with outback cattle camps on the vast, largely unfenced runs for many years. Unfortunately today, with the advent of fences and more recently mustering by air and motorbike, broncoing has just about disappeared. Broncoing was once the only way to draft, brand, earmark and cut cattle in the wide open spaces, often many miles from established cattle yards with their solid-rail races, crushes and pens.

The bronco yard consisted of a post and twisted plain-wire enclosure approximately forty metres square and about two metres high. Posts were usually of gidyea or snapping gum, but they used whatever bush timber was available in that treeless land. Off to one corner was the bronco ramp — two sturdy bush-timber rail panels in line but separated before they met by a gap large enough to take a greenhide rope. Off towards the centre of the yard was the branding fire with the irons.

Cattle were yarded and the bronco man, on a sturdy, clumper-type horse, threw the greenhide loop on to the beast to be branded and, with the aid of the horse collar to which the rope was attached, snigged it up to the ramp, slipped the rope into the gap between the two panels and continued snigging until the beast was snug against the ramp. Here it was leg-roped and thrown to the ground to be branded. In many bronco yards two horses were used, working one behind the other in a wide circle, snigging beasts up on to the ramp in turn.

"When the going was good we could put through a beast a minute," Hugh said. "But the unbranded stock were not always calves. Because of the staggering size of those unfenced western runs, clean skins could easily be missed in the muster. When they were finally yarded some of the grown 'mickeys' — unmarked bull calves — were big and wily enough to disembowel a horse if the rider was momentarily distracted."

Despite being an almost forgotten art, there are still lots of bronco yards dotted around the far west like the one we saw at Haddon Corner but they are museum pieces today, never again to see the dust and sweat or hear the curses and laughter that were part and parcel of broncoing before machine replaced flesh and blood as a beast of burden.

It's pretty sad to see the passing of an outback tradition

like the stockman, the stockhorse and the old fashioned mustering on horseback, but then it's good to be able to travel with former stockmen like Hughie who don't mind yarning about the good old stockhorse days once in a while.

"There were some exciting times in the broncoing yards," Hugh recalled as we surveyed the Haddon Corner yard. You could almost see the years rolling back before his eyes as he leaned against a once sturdy bronco ramp, now riddled with white ants.

"A lot of those clean skins were pretty big and savage when we yarded them, by crikey. Once they felt the greenhide loop drop on to them they'd put on a bit of a corroboree and it was even worse when the rope got caught under the horse and you had your horse and the mickey bucking and snorting at the same time. There was always a bit of ringers' blood spilt in the bronco yards and a lot of the time it was mine."

Only one thing wrong yarning with a bloke like Hugh Sawrey: time gets away from you before you can tell the whole story of our stay at Mt Leonard Station. Stories like the days just about half a century ago, with Hugh working for a living legend named Arthur Churches on Mooraberrie, when up to four of those huge runs, including Mt Leonard, used to combine their workforces to muster thousands of square kilometres of open country, somehow managing to sort out who owned what clean skins . . . well, almost. But that'll keep for later.

SAWREY '92

" TENDING THE " MT. LEONARD - DURRIE - MONKIRA - MOORABERRIE MUSTER "
The Pack-horse — High, Wide & Handsome
in short hobbles!

MOORABERRIE

Tending the Muster

Wide open spaces and plenty of fresh air were not the only attractions of a stockman's life on the mighty, unfenced Channel Country cattle runs when Hugh was a young ringer. There was also the glorious uncertainty of station life, not least the first time you laid eyes on the seven or eight horses allotted you by the boss. Could be a good horse among 'em. Then again they might all turn out to be real scrubbers, mad as meat-axes and ready to buck and pig-root at the drop of a hat. You just never knew.

There is a belief among city people that the stockman owned and rode his own horse, his faithful old pal. As a matter of fact about the only things a stockman owned when he arrived at a station were his swag, quartpot, saddlebag, spurs and maybe a whip. The rest, saddle, bridle and horse, were provided by the station. That was the case when Hugh took up work as a ringer for old man Churches, on Mooraberrie Station almost fifty years ago.

Mooraberrie was one of four major Channel Country stations which combined their men when it was time to muster the unfenced runs. The others were Mt Leonard, Durrie and Monkira. Together the four stations covered an area of about 21,000 square kilometres, which really is a staggering slice of the Channel Country centred on and to the east of the Diamantina River. Even today, when fences and modernisation have made mustering much easier than it used to be, the four stations still join forces in what is known as tending the muster.

Mt Leonard owner, Ashey Daley, whose company recently bought historic Cluny Station from the Holmes à Court family, gave a fair insight into the efficiency of modern methods when he explained that it used to take fourteen stockmen a fortnight to muster one 650 square kilometre area on horseback. Today, with the aid of a helicopter, seven men can do it in three days — two of them on motorbikes, the others on stockhorses. As an example of how efficient aerial mustering has become, the man who pioneered the craft, Windorah's Sandy Kidd, reckons he can muster a mob of cattle into the homestead yards from his fixed wing plane — all he needs is a bloke on the ground to shut the gate.

Back in the time I'm writing about, no one would have believed you if you said the aeroplane would one day replace the stockhorse as a means of mustering. In fact they would have said you were "illaqually" — Aboriginal for silly fella. Back then we find young Hugh surveying the seven horses just allotted to him by Mooraberrie boss, Arthur Churches. Preparing to tend the muster, Arthur had yarded a mob of new mounts purchased from central Queensland.

"A lot of the horses we got from stations 'inside' were outlaws that those stations couldn't handle," Hugh said. That's how he came face to face with a mean-looking central Queensland nag, one of two bay horses he had yet to ride, on the first day out of Mooraberrie on their way to join up with the blokes from Durrie Station.

Hugh and his stockman mate, Simsy, camped on a claypan and turned the mob of new horses out for the night in short hobbles. Simsy, whose turn it was to bring the horses on to camp at piccaninny daylight, had found that the nags had cleared out overnight and headed back for the station. Fortunately a night horse had been hobbled and tethered, so Hugh kicked the fire into action and packed up the camp ready to move, while Simsy attended to the horse tailing. The horse that had remained at camp was the meaner looking one of the two bays: he hadn't gone back with the others, probably because he wasn't used to the greenhide hobbles.

"I wasn't in any hurry to jump on him at that stage and there was no need to because the horse tailer would be back with the mob before too long," Hugh said. "But as piccaninny daylight came and went and the sun started to get higher and higher I began to worry that Simsy might have been thrown. I visualised him lying somewhere, probably with a broken leg or something."

So Hughie saddled up the bay horse and very quietly and cautiously eased himself into the saddle. "You had to be so careful with some of those horses," he said. "If you wanted to scratch your nose you very quietly drew your hand up your side taking care not to make any untoward moves."

Well, Hughie was in the saddle, and the bay's legs were splayed and shaking. Suddenly the horse snapped to attention, raced *backwards* and threw himself down in the campfire.

Hugh deserted the ship when the nag went down but found that his shirt and moleskins were smouldering in a few places. Nothing daunted, he caught and mounted the horse again, wrapped the reins around the nag's neck and said, "Righto boy! It's you or me." Again the same result — into the remains of the fire again, with Hugh bouncing out this time with smouldering gidyea coals sticking to his clothes.

"There was no way that horse didn't deliberately back into the fire both times," Hugh said. "And it did a damn good job because I had burns all over me and big holes smouldering in my pants and shirt. But I knew I had to get on that dirty bastard again if it killed me."

Fortunately just as he was preparing to mount a third time the bells of the missing mob came tinkling in from the distance with the missing stockman tailing them. A few days later Hugh got round to saddling up the second bay in his string but on the spur of the moment decided to use him as a packhorse first.

"I was half expecting a bit of a show but he remained as quiet as a mouse as I packed him. You would have sworn he was asleep. But to be on the safe side I loaded him with all I could, swags, bronco ropes, Bedourie ovens — the lot! Just then the Monkira cook sang out: 'Come and have a drink of tea you blokes.' And we were filling our pint pots out of the big billy when the packhorse snapped to attention and bucked wild-eyed through the Monkira camp, sending the other ringers in all directions then bolting across the gibber plain high, wide and handsome."

"Look at him go . . . and short-hobbled too!" yelled one of the ringers as the horse bucked about six feet in the air. "Yair!" Hughie spat. "And I could have been on the dirty orang-outang, too!"

Oh well! It was all in a day's work for a young ringer. Hugh still rides regularly and sometimes competes in "cutting" on horses bred and trained by Gill, his wife, on their quarterhorse property in the south, Bangtail Stud, home of the boot symbol brand. But these days he rarely has to pick himself out of the campfire after being dumped there by a rogue horse — at least not twice in the one morning like the good old days back on Mooraberrie.

the Swim

DIAMANTINA WAY

Ancient Haunting Wilderness

Somewhere within the intricate lacework of Diamantina River tributaries in the far west Hugh Sawrey and I stumbled on a lost paradise, the most beautiful and isolated patch of rural Queensland I've encountered. It was untouched, as if all attempts at European intrusion over the last 200 years had been invisibly repelled. Few people would have been there before us, certainly not hunters, because the animal and bird life were unconcerned as we pushed Hugh's 4WD carefully over dangerous, broken ground for mile after rough but spectacular mile.

Kangaroo — shiny Blue Fliers as well as magnificent Big Reds — paused from grazing long enough to watch us passing but held their ground and went right on feeding. Don't you love the way big red bucks stand erect, lean back on their mighty tails and square off as if to say: "Righto, mate! Come over here and try me out for size if you're game."

Poor dumb, proud fellas, those Big Reds. They've done that, squared off to man, umpteen thousand times over the years only to hear the distant crack and feel the thud, the shock, of a projectile smashing through the muscle and bone of that magnificent chest — and be gone forever. But not this time. From their lack of concern about intruders I would say no roo shooters have been along that track for many, many years; and for that reason our lost paradise will remain a secret.

We came on it by chance. Hugh was looking for a short cut and along the way we met a bloke who said we might try a bit of a track just down the road. He thought it had been graded once, but couldn't remember when. After a couple of kilometres, my guess as to when was somewhere around the time Ludwig Leichhardt and his lost legion passed that way on their fatal expedition 150 years ago.

We hadn't travelled far at all down the short cut when it almost petered out. I was all for turning back because if the next 150 kilometres were as bad as the first five then we had no hope. But I was wrong, the next 150 kilometres were much worse, just the sort of going Hughie loves because it takes him away from people, out where he can talk to the birds, the stock and the wildlife. He doesn't mind me tagging along because I don't laugh when he says a friendly "gidday" to the kookaburras or asks a lonely stockhorse how's tricks and what he thinks of the weather. The rougher and more lonely the track becomes the more Hugh likes it.

What about getting lost? Well, it helps when you know Sawrey has an uncanny bushman's nose for direction. If he hadn't we'd be just a pile of picked-over bones out near the Northern Territory border by this. Just the same, it was a real pain in the neck driving over broken black soil flats and up washed-out creekbeds for hours on end. But the inconvenience was nix when you considered that spectacular country.

On one long run through high country we passed blood-red cliffs with thickly timbered gorges slicing deep, dark and mysterious into the hills. Those cliffs stretched for miles and were pocked with caves of varying sizes — just the sort of country that might be rich in Aboriginal heritage, probably a sacred place for an ancient people. It was one of those majestic places where you feel the hairs on the back of your neck begin to prickle because you sense something special, maybe an ancient presence, close by. It's the sort of sanctity you experience standing small and insignificant deep in the Rockies or the Alps and sometimes in cathedrals like that magnificent medieval cavern in Cologne.

We yarned for a while and boiled the billy in the shadow of those catacombed cliffs and talked of unrolling our swags where we sat, maybe spending a couple of days walking through the hills. But, low to the south, dark rumbling clouds had gathered threateningly. They had appeared soon after we arrived in this high country of the red cliffs. We'd been on the side track more than four hours now and were still only half way through it. It had been one long series of black soil flats and deep, washed-out creekbeds, with the track actually running along the centre of dry creeks for kilometres. Everywhere above us old flood debris hung in tree forks, sometimes seven metres over our heads — no place to be in a flood, for sure.

I was on my second pintpot of sweet black tea, alternately looking up at the debris and back at the darkening horizon behind us, when Hugh said something that convinced me we should leave this ancient place to the spirits that doubtlessly preserve it in such ageless condition.

"Did I ever tell you about the strange wall of water that just about drowned a couple of us ringers and a mob of cattle up Monkira way?" Hughie suddenly asked, and didn't even wait for an answer. "It was the strangest thing, by cripes! Never heard of it before or since, but maybe you'll be able to ask your readers about it. I'd like to know.

"We were poking a mob of four or five hundred head of cattle across the dry Diamantina. Not a cloud in the sky, hot as blazes and dry as a bone. We became aware of a strange sound in the distance, a faint crackling. But we didn't take much notice at the time, since the horses and cattle were just walking unconcerned. The noise grew louder by the second, crackling and grinding. The only thing I've ever heard like it were the Jap bombs exploding around us in New Guinea when I was with the RAAF a couple of years before.

"It just grew and grew over a couple of minutes and

next thing a wall of water, about twelve feet high, came rolling down the creek towards us. The face of it was like grey molten lead. Broken branches and yellow spume churned out in front of it, as though some giant invisible hand had thrown Persil soap powder into it. Where one minute it was just everyday cattle work, the next second it was a swim. The cattle swam desperately and the yellow white of their eyes left an indelible impression as my nag snorted and swam, nose high in the swirling torrent.

"Both Simsy and I made it to the eastern bank and in a matter of minutes the water had gone . . .

"Yarning round the campfire that night with the Monkira ringers the general opinion was that there had been a cloudburst upriver maybe a hundred kilometres or more a couple of days previously."

By this stage my untouched pintpot of tea had gone stone cold and there was a distinct pain in my neck from my head swivelling between the flood debris seven metres up a nearby gum tree to the black clouds rumbling ominously out of the south. Up in the cliffs those ancient, blood-red caves and their Dreamtime secrets beckoned with power and mystery. But they were not even in the race against the power of my fear of being caught in a wall of boiling water spiked with whirling logs and heck knows what else. So we went.

Somewhere around closing time that night we stumbled into an isolated pub for a couple of stiff rums — without water, thanks. One day I'd like to go back to that lost paradise and look through those caves and gorges; but I can't help thinking the ancient spirits that seem to guard them may conjure up a little more mischief to keep the traveller moving on.

"a chip of the old block"
James Kidd
— Windorah S.W. Qld.

SAWREY

WINDORAH

Revolution in Cattle Country

With a population of sixty-five citizens and two poddy calves that live in the main street, Windorah is not the kind of hamlet you would associate with the birth of an industrial revolution. Sure, it's neat and green in an otherwise brown land, the way most far western towns are these days with their reticulated water systems. But since Paddy Gordon's general store stopped selling mouth organs some time back, things have been positively slow.

Once upon a time Paddy used to sell lots of harmonicas to passing ringers and drovers, but mainly to the one female customer. That's where the trouble started. You see, local drinkers at the Western Star Hotel reckon she was the worst mouth organ player in the entire world, only she didn't know it. Thought she was Larry Adler's highly gifted sister, hey? She used to drive drinkers crazy, blasting tunelessly away between drinks, until one night they came up with a pretty sneaky idea. They hid her mouth organ when she went down the back for a couple of secs and she never found it again.

Next night she was back in the bar with another mouth organ, purchased that day from Paddy's place right across the road. They hid that one too which she never found either. The next night she lost another new mouth organ, and the next night another.

Well, townsfolk in places like Windorah can be fairly persuasive and today Paddy's general store doesn't stock mouth organs. You can get needles and thread, headache cures, saddles, blankets, food and clothing, even kitchen sinks . . . it's a little ripper of a general store. But you can't get a mouth organ for love nor money. Until Hugh Sawrey lobbed into town recently they hadn't heard a mouth organ in the Western Star in months and I reckon after we left they won't want to hear another one in a long, long time because Hughie blew up such a storm in the pub one night their ears will still be ringing.

When you can play as well as Hughie, though, no one minds; in fact, they all want to join in, so it's a great way to meet new mates. That's exactly how we met the man who put Windorah on the map as the birthplace of an industrial revolution.

Sandy Kidd, fifty-two, rough and tumble, smiling around a skinny makings and yelling with a voice like river gravel rattling off the back of an old tip-truck, is the father of aerial mustering, a method that has revolutionised the grazing industry. Now aerial mustering may not mean much to townsfolk, but over the last generation it has jolted the industry out of horse and buggy days right into the jet age. Without the transition from traditional horseback mustering, first to fixed wing planes and now to helicopters, the grazing industry would be a lot worse off than it is today, probably facing terminal disaster.

Unfortunately there is a human cost to this progress. Gone are the stockmen of old — stockmen like Hugh Sawrey, stockmen in their thousands always in great demand on stations big and small from the Channel Country to the Gulf, from Queensland to Western Australia. Alas, the stockman has all but passed into legend in the nineties. Thank God that Sawrey had a vision splendid back in the seventies that will be his legacy to future generations of otherwise ignorant Australians — the Stockman's Hall of Fame. The Hall is Hugh's baby.

On our entire 3300 kilometre journey through the Channel Country and beyond we spotted only one horseman. He was riding through Cunnamulla, probably ambling down to the corner store for a take-away pizza and a home video, for all I know.

The silver lining to that cloud of progress is the modern miracle that greatly helped the grazing industry — aerial mustering. And, like many important technological breakthroughs, it happened by chance during severe floods back in 1963. Even back then Sandy Kidd was something of a legend not only for his outstanding rescue work, his safety record, and his skilled seat-of-the-pants flying, but also his knowledge of the far southwest corner of Queensland. Even in his early teens Sandy was taken on board commercial flights by pilots not familiar with the country to help with visual navigation. In the years since, many private pilots have owed him great debts of gratitude, if not their lives, because he has become a human beacon for pilots straying off course in the vast southwest.

"If a pilot loses his way out here I can usually put him back on track if he can tell me by radio what he can see down below," Sandy rasped. It might be a range over there, a windmill here and a water course in the distance, but Sandy will know the exact spot. After all he has been flying that country for more than thirty-five years.

Being the owner of one of the few light planes in the southwest he flew long hours dropping tucker to stranded station workers and stock in the 1963 flood. A lot of that rescue work took him over the wide flood plains where the Thompson and Barcoo Rivers meet north of Windorah. Stock were stranded there in thousands. Sandy flew over one mob of 1600 head, almost submerged, and knew they were doomed because they could not be physically moved to higher ground just a few miles away. He could see it all from the cockpit. It was impossible to get to them on horseback and the owner had already written them off as a flood loss. But Sandy wouldn't accept defeat. He decided to try to frighten them towards higher ground by buzzing low over the back of the mob. To his surprise they started moving ever so slowly in the desired direction.

"I was making lots of trips up and down the river on rescue work at that stage and flew over the stranded mob often. So each time I swooped down and buzzed them again just to keep them moving," he said.

The mob kept on moving and eventually reached the safety of high ground. Only seven head of the doomed 1600 were lost. When the flood waters subsided Sandy reckoned he would do a little experimental aerial mustering on his 57,000 hectare sheep and cattle property, Ourdel, a couple of miles outside Windorah. It worked, and over the coming years he perfected aerial mustering to an art form where, as I said earlier, all he needed was someone on the ground to shut the gate when he mustered the mob into the homestead yards. "If there is a strip near the yards I can do it all myself. I just land, race over on foot, and slam the gate," he said.

Today, almost thirty years on, mustering by fixed wing aircraft is becoming as old hat as mustering on horseback. Helicopters are all the go, but that doesn't mean the Kidd family is out in the cold. Sandy's son, James "Dood" Kidd, is a helicopter pilot operating as an aerial mustering contractor throughout the Channel Country.

"My grandfather came to this country on horseback a hundred and two years ago," said Sandy, rather wistfully for the gravel-voiced bloke he is. "I'd love to know what he would say if he could see us today, his grandson mustering in a light plane and his great-grandson mustering in a helicopter."

Yep! It is a rather interesting question. I'd say the long-gone old bloke would be pretty proud. What do you reckon?

GEORGE QUART-POT — POLICE TRACKER.

SAWREY '92.

Once a Billy Boy...

George Quartpot is a very special man, the last of his tribe, in fact — the last of the fair dinkum black trackers in Queensland's trackless far southwest. He's retired now, at seventy-five, but when he tracked, his Dreamtime craft defied the wonders of modern technology. It saved lives where sophisticated search parties stood pondering their next best guess. It brought criminals to justice over terrain that would barbecue a bloodhound.

George's voice is just about gone now, all worn out from a lifetime spent in or near the desert. He talks in the faintest whisper, so if you want to hear wisdom born out of the maybe 40,000 years of Dreamtime tradition you have to bend really close to that noble face. Thus was I inclined recently in Boulia, ears straining, waiting for an answer that might give me a better understanding of the unbridged gap between his race, his generation — and mine.

What had he learned in a lifetime wandering from Alice Springs to Woorabinda as tribesman, drover, ringer and tracker? What was the one lesson he had learned from such a fathomless traditional life? George Quartpot's gaze soared off to the horizon and I waited patiently, breathlessly. Eventually his lips began to move and I crouched even closer, afraid to miss a single syllable. The answer was almost inaudible.

"I wish . . . I wish I could find tucker as quick as that

Bush Tucker fella on television," he said. "It always took me a long time to find tucker. And it's hard to spear kangaroo. He too quick."

George reckons it would have saved him a hell of a lot of time over the years because he's always been a fair dinkum bush tucker man, and even today he still bowls over an occasional goanna for the campfire. Boulia store-keeper Cliff Donohue reckons George complained recently there were not as many goannas around Boulia as in old times. Cliff told him that wasn't correct because his customers were always complaining about goannas raiding their chook houses. "Ah yes," said George. "That's because *alura agura* (big sand goanna) know white fella won't eat him. But he hides from us black fellas, hey?"

Although George has spent much of his life in bush towns or on stations in the far west and the Territory, he has never lost touch with his traditional roots. Until recently he went walkabout yearly from Boulia hundreds of kilometres west into the Toko Ranges and the Territory. He and Tibby and their family lived off the land for long periods and made corroboree with friendly Aborigines they met along the way.

George is not too clear on his early life but believes he was born into the Arunda tribe somewhere in the Territory in August 1917. He believes his family name was Beauchamp. He inherited his present surname from his first job as billy boy to a boundary rider because he was always yelling out "Quartpot" when the billy boiled. He says over the years he's been called Barney, Archie and many other names, some not too pleasant, but decided to call himself George many years ago and still thinks it's a pretty good handle.

Not surprisingly life hasn't showered George Quartpot with riches, but he's better off today than he was when he started work in his early teens. At that stage he hadn't heard of wages. He worked for tucker and keep, boundary riding, dogging, even droving goats, and hardly knew what money was. He reckons he was almost twenty before he received his first pay when he joined a drover named

Paddy Davoren in Boulia. Paddy was taking a mob of cattle from Glengyle Station, outside Bedourie, down the Birdsville Track to Clayton Station in South Australia. George doesn't remember how long it took but by modern road map it's more than 600 kilometres one way through some of Australia's harshest and most unforgiving wilderness. When they got back to Boulia Paddy handed George his first pay of ten bob, a dollar in today's money. It seemed like a great deal in those days — George reckoned that was the life for him. He stayed with Paddy for several years droving in the Channel Country.

His next job was working sheep on Strathelbis Station and here he first came under the far-off city bureaucrats' parental care. He became a signed-up member of the Aboriginal Welfare Fund — which appears to have been a great fund for the state government and its bureaucrats but not so good for people like Mr Quartpot, who earned the pittance handed out to black fellas in those days.

This is how the fund worked for George Quartpot, black tracker, anyway. When he signed on in the late thirties, George was paid 11 bob ($1.10) a week by the station owner. Of this, six bob went into the fund for safekeeping and the rest went to George in hard cash for living expenses. I'd like to think old George still has something in kitty in the fund, but I'd say not.

Anyway, in 1950 George was appointed Boulia's official black tracker and one of his early jobs was saving the lives of a young girl and boy who had disappeared from Roxborough Station. He reckons one of his toughest jobs was tracking down a tribesman named Pudden-Head Tommy who took off into the desert for no good reason. George tracked him for kilometres through Glenormiston Station out near the Territory border but suddenly his tracks disappeared into thin air. George said Pudden-Head somehow discovered he was tracking him and put on a pair of kadaitcha shoes he'd made on the run, thus hiding his tracks. (Kadaitcha shoes are made of human hair, blood, string and feathers, and are designed to hide footprints.) There was little George and the police could do after that so they abandoned the search, never expecting to see Pudden-Head again. But some months later Pudden-Head walked out of the desert to join friendly tribes in the Territory.

George reckons he's got no quarrel with us white fellas except for one bloke about thirty-five years ago. It was his boss, a policeman, and they had a falling out over George's wages. George asked for a rise, see. But George thinks he may have lost that argument because soon after the barney he lost his tracking job at Boulia and was sent east to Woorabinda settlement where he became a garbageman.

Today, back in Boulia in retirement, George Quartpot has turned his talents to medicine, but his one cure-it-all label, "Doggie Bush Oil", is not for patients with weak stomachs. In fact it smells rather crook, even with the lid firmly on. And if Major Les Hiddins (ret.) happens to read this, would he mind telling Tracker Quartpot (ret.) how to catch bush tucker real quick like he does on TV? It will make a very special old man real happy.

The Royal Mail *South to Glengyle*

BOULIA — BEDOURIE

Royal Mail Service
No. 276

Eddie Miller, overseer of Royal Mail Service No. 276 and the last of the Boulia mailmen, had a pretty easy job on paper. All he had to do was load his truck with mail, provisions and passengers in Boulia on Thursday, drive 247 kilometres south to Glengyle Station, stopping overnight at Bedourie, and return to Boulia on Saturday arvo — a paltry round trip of 494 kilometres and three whole days in which to do it. But you don't get the real picture until you learn that the roads in Eddie's day were pretty crook, and that was in an extremely good season. In fact some were not much better when Sawrey and I travelled them recently.

Eddie used to tell the story of another old Channel Country mailman and his passenger driving through a blinding dust storm at night and the passenger asking how the hell the mailman knew where the road was. "When I get on to some smooth going I know I'm off the road for sure," was his reply. One thing can be said of Eddie the mailman: if only half of modern Australia's bosses and workers applied the same uncomplaining diligence as he did to Royal Mail Service No. 276, this country would not be in the mess it is in today.

The late Eddie Miller was an honest man who believed in sticking at his job until it was done because there were few excuses given or expected in those days; and he was a fair representative of many western workers of his time. He knew his job and nothing got in his road going about it. But don't take my word for it, let former Bedourie and Birdsville policeman, Eric Sammon, now retired, describe the first time he bumped into Eddie "Jolly" Miller back in February 1943.

Eric had just been transferred from Brisbane to Bedourie and joined Eddie's mail truck for the trip from Boulia. He was surprised when Eddie advised him to pack a swag and a bit of tucker for the six hour trip. Three days later, hungry, wet and covered in mud, Eric, Eddie and Royal Mail Service No. 276 were still on the road in circumstances Eric recalls vividly nearly fifty years on, but which were just part of the day-to-day job for Eddie the mailman.

Their trouble started about sixty kilometres out of Boulia where two channels of the Georgina River were in flood and looked impassable to the new policeman, who was ready to return to Boulia and wait for better times. But Eddie simply pulled off the fan belt, covered the engine with a waterproof sheet, ploughed through the first channel and repeated the process at the second channel a kilometre down the muddy track. Well, if the Georgina channels looked impassable to Eric, he was incredulous thirty kilometres further on when the mailman made light of crossing five channels of Bellevue Creek. Eddie put chains on the rear dual wheels, had Eric place two-metre-long planks under them and crawled forward two metres at a time, with the policeman bringing the planks forward each time the rear wheels progressed that far.

Progress was slow but steady until they reached the middle of the first channel when the planks and wheels disappeared to the axles. No bother, said Eddie examining this disaster. He simply unloaded the truck, which was carrying about two and a half tons of mail and stores, recovered the planks from the mud and tied them cross-ways across the rear wheels. By this method Eddie was able to drive the truck forward about half a metre at a time, before untying them and shifting them back to their original position so he could move the truck forward another half a metre. Sounds mighty slow? You bet it was, but the truck was moving in the right direction, and anyway, Eric recalls, Eddie was going about it like it was just a normal part of the job — he was to learn it *was* a normal part of the mailman's job in the wet season.

At eight o'clock that first night the mail truck was over the first channel and Eddie called it a day. They camped beside the truck. They were up early next day and, with little to eat, went straight into the same routine. By eight o'clock that night they had crossed the fifth channel, unloading the truck and inching forward about half a metre a time all through the day and into the night. They camped beside the truck for the second night. At day-break the third day they reloaded the truck and set off on the last leg to Bedourie, only to be held up by more flooded channels, which were crossed once again by unloading the truck and fastening the planks crossways over the rear wheels. That night at nine o'clock, they arrived in Bedourie and, as Eric recalls, forgot their troubles with a couple of strong drinks.

Of course troubles were far from over for the mailman because he still had to return to Boulia the same way he came down, this time without the help of passengers. And when he got back to Boulia he turned round, loaded up and did it all over again. Those blokes not only delivered mail through thick and thin, they brought the latest news by word of mouth, often the only contact some of those lonely stations had in the days before radio and telephone communications had reached outlying regions.

Some far western stations were still waiting for a telephone connection with the outside world when Hugh Sawrey and I were out there earlier this year. And as Eddie's widow, May, told me in Boulia at the time, in the loneliness of the outback, mail day was a red letter day for isolated people, particularly women.

"The arrival of the mailman was a two-way morale booster because their delight at seeing and talking to Eddie about what was happening in the outside world gave him great satisfaction and made the endless miles he covered seem very worthwhile," she said. "Eddie brought them letters from their children away at boarding school and also shopping catalogues. Those were the days when station women did their shopping by catalogue from the big city stores. Imagine their delight on receiving those colorful catalogues with the latest fashions!"

Quite often the mailman was called on to help out with odd jobs on shorthanded properties, helping with cattle yards and even the housework. May remembers the time Eddie was asked to help Bill, an outstation manager, kill a beast for butchering. With no yards, the man with the rifle, Eddie, sat silently in a tree waiting for Bill to move the small mob of wild cattle, including the "killer", to a convenient spot under the tree. Cattle never look up so it is easy to drop the killer with a single shot, as long as the mob are not frightened by noise or sudden movement. Well, Bill poked the killer and the small mob right under the tree the postman sat in, motionless and waiting.

The mob settled down, all quiet like, the mailman slowly raised the rifle, then lowered it and shouted: "Which one do you want me to shoot, Bill, eh?" That's the last they saw of the killer and the rest of the mob, so they went without meat for the next week or two.

When Eddie Miller died at Redcliffe in 1991 a slice of the Queensland outback went with him because he really was the last of the Boulia mailmen. These days a plane delivers the mail on Eddie's old Boulia–Bedourie run because they couldn't get anyone game enough to replace him on the road with Royal Mail Service No. 276.

"The Min-Min light"

BOULIA

Seeing the Light

A dull twang disturbed the dry western air as Sawrey flicked the thin metal strip he'd just recovered from the last earthly remains of the Min Min Hotel outside Boulia. Rusting metal harness fittings and broken and melted glass were scattered across the site of the old hotel, no doubt picked over by travellers like us many times in the estimated seventy-four years since the building burnt down. It was a very interesting place by a dry creek in the stony plain. Rusty matchboxes, old buckles, metal rings, iron hoops from kegs and wagon wheels were everywhere, but Hugh had happened on the one thin metal strip in the ruins.

He considered it for a minute or so, twanging it dully, his artist's inner eye looking at the options for, who knows, a future masterpiece . . . "This'd be a stay from the flash barmaid's corset," he said finally and you could bet there was inspiration here for a bold and bright scene of a buxom wench pulling buckets of beer for a thirsty mob of wild-eyed colonials. Still, it was extremely hard to imagine a flash, corseted barmaid ever having worked in this hot, dry place, the more so in a slab shanty that served as a trap to lonely travellers — late last century it had a reputation for stunning ringers with rotgut brew before separating them from their pay cheques.

It was one more tantalising tidbit to an eerie, desolate landscape that was the birthplace of Australia's greatest phenomenon and one still without explanation, the Min

Min Light. That's why we were among the Min Min ruins recently, hoping to see what all the fuss was about, maybe even see the Light. But when your mate starts talking about a flash barmaid's corsets and there's still eight hours of daylight left, you know it's time to move on. Besides, there was a chance to camp at Combo Waterhole that night, a hallowed place for a Banjo Paterson fan, and we were two.

It was by Combo Hole, just east of Kynuna, that the Banjo was inspired to write "Waltzing Matilda". So it wasn't a hard decision to make. We travelled on, leaving the stay from the flash barmaid's corset to rest in peace among the ruins. As it turned out it was one of our worst decisions because that very night the Min Min Light made one of its rare appearances down the road from the old ruins where we would have unrolled our swags.

Local grazier Bruiser Cooms and a young ringer were returning from Winton to Boulia when the Light appeared. According to Cooms it was a typical show by the Light, a bright beam in the distance off the beaten track, suddenly appearing in the darkness, burning bright, about the size of a football, approaching at first then retreating into the distance.

"I've seen it before and there was no mistaking it that night," Cooms said. "It frightened hell out of the young bloke. He wanted to take off. If you blokes had camped at the ruins you probably would have seen it too. We would have dragged you out of your swags anyway." That would have been unnerving in itself because Bruiser Cooms from Burglar Downs looks exactly as a bloke named Bruiser Cooms from Burglar Downs should look — big and mighty tough. But as big and tough as Mr Cooms is, he is unshaken in his belief in the Min Min Light, as are locals in the Boulia–Winton area where the Light is most likely to appear.

Although science has failed to explain this ghostly manifestation, it is nevertheless real to the hundreds, perhaps thousands, of people who have seen it.

Over the years local daredevils have taken pot shots at

it and even suffered severe injuries in falls from their horses when, full of booze, they've charged flat strap into the night, hoping to run it down like a scrub bull. Local storekeeper Cliff Donohue, a former Boulia shire chairman, had to counsel shocked shire workers terrorised by the Light while camped on the road. His father Jim, a pioneering bullocky in the district, became lost several times after following the Min Min Light, believing it to be his distant campfire.

"In those days the teams would pass up good feed to camp by good water at night," Cliff said. "When they had unhitched and watered their bullocks they would walk them back, sometimes miles, to good feed they had passed on the road that day. They always built big campfires near their wagons to find their way back, but a couple of times my dad mistook the Min Min Light for his fire and ended up hopelessly lost."

Although the Min Min Light is believed to have been seen many years before, the first reported sighting, recorded in Boulia's centenary book, was around 1918 in a graveyard behind the burnt out Min Min Hotel. The only identifiable grave there today is that of Mary Lilley, wife of W.T.C. Lilley, a tank sinker who built the shanty in about 1886.

A stockman riding from Lucknow Station to Boulia was passing the ruins of the hotel about ten p.m. one night when he saw a light hovering over the graveyard, took fright and spurred off towards Boulia with the light in hot pursuit. His report was incoherent when he arrived at the Boulia police station 108 kilometres later, but when he was able to tell his tale it was taken as a joke.

A few nights later a stockman and his wife reported a similar light at the Min Min ruins. They were unaware of the first report and after seeing the strange glow, they turned on to the plain to follow it. It kept moving away, and they lost interest but as they turned back towards the road, the Light began to follow them. They reported the incident to Boulia police, much to the relief of the stockman who first reported the Light.

Since then many locals and travellers have seen it over a wide area, but mainly in the vicinity of the Min Min hotel ruins. It has been variously attributed to natural gases escaping from the earth, fungal growth, swarming fire-flies, phosphorescent night birds and the supernatural. Scientists have examined it and priests have investigated it, but the Min Min Light remains the mystery it was the night it frightened the living daylights out of the Lucknow stockman.

Until I took this trip to Min Min I hadn't thought one way or the other about the Light although I had heard the story from a very early age. But after talking to old hands around the far west I believe people do occasionally see a light that is, at this stage, beyond explanation. It's more than a campfire tale and one which may have become a reality for me if my mate hadn't started dreaming about the stays from a flash barmaid's corset among the ruins of the old Min Min shanty. Was that a good reason to move on or what?

By the Combo waterhole

KYNUNA

Waltzing Matilda by Combo Waterhole

You couldn't call yourself a dinkum Aussie if you un-rolled your swag and boiled your billy by Combo Waterhole on a mild and starry night without bellowing at least one chorus of "Waltzing Matilda". Thus were the famous Combo coolibahs, and all the dinky-di inhabitants nestled therein, startled out of their sleep one night when the plaintive notes of Hugh Sawrey's harmonica drifted over those still, yellow waters . . . the more so when in raspy tones I joined in the song that is Australia:

> Who'll come a-waltzing Matilda, my darling?
> Who'll come a-waltzing Matilda with me?
> Waltzing Matilda and leading a water-bag,
> Who'll come a-waltzing Matilda with me?

After all, this ordinary looking waterhole just east of Kynuna and 1530 kilometres northwest of Brisbane has been pinpointed as the spot where A.B."Banjo" Paterson was inspired to write the words of the famous song — rather ordinary words I might add — to a pleasant melody which has become Australia's internationally known song; one day it might be our national anthem, who knows?

What is it about a song that tells the story of a bagman who pinches a sheep, is caught redhanded by the troopers and suicides by jumping into a billabong? Not a theme to inspire a nation, I'll be bound; not the way "Matilda" has. Nevertheless, on a fathomless starry night like the one when I was at Combo Hole, the story can take on a special aura, certainly enough to inspire the artist in my friend.

We were sitting on our swags in the campfire's glow while Hughie vamped "Matilda" like a dirge. You could almost see the Banjo's countenance dancing in the flicker, and hear the clopping hooves of troopers one, two, three. It was eerie. The harmonica notes had barely died across the water when a long and plaintive cry echoed down the billabong. Hugh turned to me and whispered: "What was that? A night bird . . . or was it the swagman pleading for release from the muddy waters?" Cripes! I didn't know, nor did I want to know. I wanted to crawl into my swag and pull the Birkmire cover over my head. It's the only place to be when the bunyips are out and about like that night by Combo Hole.

It is indeed a haunted place on a deep, dark night. Maybe the spooks were also abroad ninety-seven years ago when Paterson was there with a picnic party while on holidays at nearby Dagworth Station, where he stayed for several weeks with his Winton fiancée, Sarah Wiley — chaperoned of course. Several days after the picnic, in January 1895, he wrote "Waltzing Matilda". It was a particularly lively time in the west thanks to the shearers' strike, and especially at Dagworth, which had been in the thick of things. You can be sure Paterson's mind was cluttered with weird and wonderful tales heaped on him by locals at the picnic, and in the days leading up to the poem.

Just a couple of months earlier Dagworth had been the scene of a fierce gun battle between striking shearers and the owners, the Macpherson family. It was a well-planned attack by the shearers who were intent on destroying the woolshed before the Macphersons could begin shearing. The man detailed to set fire to the shed, "Frenchy" Hoffmeister, did a good job under covering fire from his friends, but was to regret ever striking the match. Unknown to him there were 140 weaners and lambs trapped inside. The horror of his actions was too much for Hoffmeister. He blew his brains out soon after at a Diamantina waterhole about twelve kilometres upstream from where we camped at Paterson's picnic spot.

It does not take much imagination to speculate that the battle and suicide were told in great detail to Paterson when the Dagworth residents gave one of their regular picnics at Combo, a central recreational spot for Dagworth and neighbouring Kynuna Station. Nor would it have been unusual for the talk to include a curse or two for the bloody bagmen and out-of-work shearers who regularly bowled over local squatters' sheep for a leg of mutton or two.

One day while out riding, Bob Macpherson showed Paterson a dead sheep with a hind leg missing but cunningly laid out as if it had died of natural causes. Macpherson cursed the waste, pointing out he would give swaggies mutton if they would only ask. Paterson was also known to have seen and passed comment on the grave of an old wool scourer, George Pope, who staggered drunk into a waterhole and drowned on Dagworth in 1891. Into this scrabble of events weave a pleasant melody that had captured Paterson since he first heard it played on the autoharp by Christina Macpherson on his arrival at Dagworth. It was a Scottish tune called "Craigielee". Christine in turn had heard it played by a brass band at far-off Warrnambool races and committed it to memory.

Outback author Richard Magoffin, who has thoroughly researched "Matilda's" history, believes a dinner conversation of routine station events focused Paterson's mind to bring all these events together to accompany Christina's tune. Asked over dinner what he had seen that day, Dagworth overseer, Jack Carter, is said to have replied: "Nothing much, only a bagman waltzing Matilda down along the river." Paterson was intrigued because he had never heard the term "waltzing Matilda", a common label for carrying your swag in both Victoria and Queensland in those days, but not in Paterson's Sydney. After dinner Paterson asked Christina to play her Warrnambool tune again and before they snuffed out the lanterns on old Dagworth Station that night, "Waltzing Matilda" had been born.

Paterson's three week sojourn at Dagworth ended soon after and he and Sarah travelled back to Winton, chaperoned again naturally. During a short stay with Sarah's family in Winton, Paterson heard "Waltzing Matilda" sung in public for the first time by grazier Herbert Ramsay at the North Gregory Hotel. Soon after, the song was being passed on by word of mouth, more or less, into Australian folklore. Paterson headed back to his law practice, almost certainly unaware that he had just created an Australian tradition that would stand as long as there is breath in the last fair dinkum Australian.

As Hugh and I looked at our old billy boiling by Combo Hole recently, we sang with gusto under those magnificent Combo coolibah trees, and I estimate there will be a few more Aussie generations doing the same for a few more centuries to come.

BOULIA

Women of the Outback

There wouldn't be a job in the great Queensland out-back that women haven't tackled since Europeans first pushed out there a century and a half ago. The same cannot be said of outback men — or at least I have yet to hear of the lowly ringer or even the head serang bearing children, let alone raising them in a hostile environment. Thousands of women faced the same daily hardships as men, but with the added burden of bringing up nippers, sometimes a dozen or more.

My grandmother had thirteen kids, the first, my old man, born late last century in the central Queensland bush. We loved her but didn't think her personal trial of bringing up thirteen children, some of them in a slab hut with a dirt floor and camp oven cooking in a lean-to, was anything special. And in a way it wasn't, because that was just something you expected bush women of pioneering days to do. I might add that pioneering conditions exist today in some outlying districts, even pretending this recession isn't happening.

My grandma was probably one of the lucky ones be-cause she at least had a roof over her head when many like her were living in tents and wagons on the track with their men, following work. Outside Boulia on oh-so-lonely Min Min Creek in an unkempt grave lie the bones of Mary Lilley, mother of eight and dead at fifty-nine. Hers is a remarkable story today, yet the more I move around this state the more I realise she was just an ordinary sort of woman doing what came naturally in those days, sticking by her man through thick and thin.

Mary would have been in her early 40s and expecting her eighth child when her teamster husband W.T.C. Lilley decided to leave Beaufort on the Victorian goldfields to seek work as a tank sinker around the new western Queensland hamlet of Boulia. It wasn't a big deal. All he had to do was pack his tank sinking equipment, months of provisions and his worldly possessions into his bullock wagon, pile his pregnant wife and seven kids on top of that and travel almost 3000 kilometres across a largely trackless continent.

On 11 June 1880, somewhere along the track between Wagga Wagga and the Griffith district, Mary gave birth to her last child, Lucy (who incidentally only died back in 1972). After more than six months on the track they arrived at Boulia to become pioneers of the district.

Amazingly such a dangerous overland trek from Victoria to Queensland was not uncommon last century. Many Victorians took up vast tracts of land in far western Queensland and some even pressed on to north Queensland and right up Cape York. Of course some made it, others didn't. They died of fevers and diseases, perished in day-to-day accidents, starved, or were speared by Aborigines defending their land.

The Lilleys made it and old W.T.C. did well in his tank sinking business, during which time his wife and family lived in tents and at the tank sites. He also established several cattle stations and in the late 1880s built the lonely Min Min Hotel on the track from Boulia to Winton where Mary lies today. But even at the "hotel" life was not easy for Mary Lilley. It was a slab shanty and a pretty rough one at that, according to contemporary reports, with frequent brawls between station workers cutting out their pay cheques for rotgut brews. The famed Min Min Light, which takes it name from the pub, is reported to have first been seen near Mary's grave, close to the pub ruins.

Not a great deal is known about Mary's day-to-day

existence a century ago, but it's like a weighty tome compared to the secret life of a flame-haired stockwoman known around far western Queensland as Red Jack. She appeared out of the bush, tall and gaunt, astride a black stallion near Hughenden a year after Mary Lilley died in 1897. But more of Red Jack later.

Still, all the interesting women of the Outback have not passed into history. Certainly not Edna Jessop (née Zigenbine), boss drover, horse breaker and, until recently, pound keeper at Mount Isa for the last twenty-six years. Old timers told me Edna always called a spade a bloody shovel in her droving days on the stock routes of the Northern Territory and Queensland so I wasn't disappointed when I asked her about her pound-keeping job.

"The rotten bludgers retired me in April just because I'm sixty-five years old and I broke my bloody arm," rasped Edna. "The broken arm didn't stop me riding or doing the job. It's a bit bent that's all, but it wouldn't stop me doing the job for another year at least. I asked for another year. I even saw the bloody mayor. But they just retired me."

In another era I reckon Edna would have taken a stockwhip to the blokes who did her out of her job. But the good old droving days are all over now. Edna was born in 1927, one of eight children raised in droving camps by their parents, Ruby and Harry Zigenbine. She never went to school but was taught to read and write by her mother.

"I had a wonderful mum and dad," Edna said, softly now she was talking about more pleasant things. "They were great parents. They used to battle for us. Poor mum . . . the poor old thing. I often lay awake at night wondering how she coped the way she did. She had my young sister Mavis under a bough shed on the track."

The way Edna talks about her own time as a drover you'd think her life was a bed of roses, but she spent almost a quarter of a century on the track droving, many of them as the boss — waking hours in the saddle and sleeping in a swag in all weather. Her droving trips sometimes covered more than 2000 kilometres. Far removed from Edna's droving days but covering the same vast distances in an era that is as remote from hers as a wagon is from an aeroplane, is another woman who I'm sure would cringe at being labelled an outback pioneer. Roman Catholic nun, Sister Anne Maree Jensen, of the Aerial Ministry Service, Longreach, is just that, however. For eleven months of the year the Toowoomba-born nun flies a four-seater Cessna 172 into seven townships and more than fifty stations in a 250,000 square kilometre area of western Queensland, reaching as far as Birdsville. Half the time she travels alone, the other half with a priest to say Mass in the outback outposts. There she visits the sick and the lonely, and prepares outback children for the Sacraments.

"Mainly I do a lot of talking and a lot of listening," she said. "It is a very enriching occupation because there are a lot of people . . . a lot of women . . . out there who are very isolated and don't get the chance to talk to outsiders."

It is a unique career Sister Anne Maree never imagined for herself when she began teaching as a nun in Brisbane in 1979. She later taught in Emerald before moving to Longreach from 1985 until 1987 where she first came in contact with the aerial ministry, although at that stage she had no plans to fly an aeroplane. But after transfer to Maroochydore in 1988 she was asked if she would learn to fly and return to Longreach to take over the aerial ministry. "I had a licence to drive a car and truck so I thought, why not a plane?" she said.

Since then she has flown a total of almost 1000 hours around the west, clocking up 300 flying hours a year, which is quite a change for a young nun who hadn't even thought of flying an aeroplane as a hobby three years before, let alone accepting a job which involved flying solo over some of Australia's most remote and forbidding territory. To her it's a job that has to be done, no doubt every bit as demanding yet spiritually rewarding as those of the mothers who helped pioneer the Outback through all kinds of adversity because it was simply something that had to be done. Women really have tackled every job in the outback — and one in particular that will never be matched by the men, not by the lowliest ringer or even the most powerful head serang.

SAWREY

"Red Jack"

HUGHENDEN

That Woman, Red Jack

Graveyards are full of our heritage; trouble is most of it is irredeemably locked in the dead and unrecorded memories among our ancestors' bones. We are all to blame. Each of us should be responsible for recording our old people's memories before they too take their small slice of history to the grave. It can be a thankless, repetitious task, don't I know! But occasionally snippets of forgotten tales of unusual people and events come to light that could be the makings of a bestseller.

The life and times of Red Jack, stockwoman, horse-breaker, tragic mother, but above all a loner on the far western cattle runs, is the stuff of bestsellers. Unfortunately most of her life in the west is buried with the old people who must have occasionally come in contact with her when she worked as a man, astride a black stallion named Mephistopheles, around the turn of this century.

Recorded history may never have heard of this flame-haired woman had it not been for a tantalising entry in the diary of a pioneer cattleman, Michael Durack, about a brief meeting he had with her on a Cobb and Co. coach track outside Hughenden ninety-four years ago. Durack, from one of Australia's best-known early grazier families, was a passenger on the coach in July 1898 when Red Jack rode out of the bush. About his trip from Camooweal to the south, he later wrote in his diary: "One person encountered on my journey is worthy of special comment — a woman, tall, gaunt-looking and with bright red hair, who helped us rummage for her mail before riding away."

Durack asked locals about the stockwoman, only to be told that her name was unknown (except for the sobriquet Red Jack), she was an experienced stockwoman, she shunned company and her only friend appeared to be her black stallion Mephistopheles.

Not a lot of information there, but enough to leave Hugh Sawrey and me thirsting for more when we read the diary entry in Longreach at the Stockman's Hall of Fame. It was enough inspiration also for Durack's daughter, Dame Mary Durack, author of the bestseller *Kings in Grass Castles*, to dedicate a poem to Red Jack more than fifty years later:

> And strange the tales they told of them
> Who ranged the dusty track,
> The great black Mephistopheles
> And the red-haired witch, Red Jack.

So little was recorded about Red Jack that several knowledgable westerners I spoke to questioned her existence. But back in Brisbane, with the help of researcher Helen Hamley, Red Jack came to life as a tragic, bedevilled individual. No doubt her tragic early life caused her to seek solitude in the harsh wide open spaces of the outback working as a stockman from the time of her jealous husband's suicide in 1891 to her own death in 1902. So this is the known story of the woman they called Red Jack.

She was born Hannah Glennon on a small farm on the Darling Downs on 18 July,1872. It was a poor farm at best, and circumstances were made worse when, following a period of blindness, her father John died. Her mother remarried but the stepfather soon died, followed by her mother, leaving young Hannah and her brother Bill to scratch out a living. Probably for economic reasons Bill left the farm, working as a stockman and horse-breaker out west and returning to the farm from time to time with mobs of horses which he and Hannah broke in on the farm.

A common thread in the limited contemporary accounts of her life is the fact that Red Jack was an outstanding horsewoman who rode astride the horse like a man, which must have been unusual in the days when genteel women only rode side-saddle. One report of her riding ability gave unstinting praise: "One day in the home yard I saw her ride in breeches, boots and spurs. The horse was a low-set, short-backed, strong-boned animal, said to have been sent from the Lockyer district just to try Hannah out. He had already thrown the best riders on the Lockyer, and Black Peter Rouse from the Logan.

"She saddled him in the ring yard. Getting the reins righted, Hannah took a lug hold on him and landed on his back like a fly and rammed the spurs into him. The outlaw held his wind, giving seven or eight vicious bucks and, pulling up to get his wind, he made two more desperate attempts to unseat his rider. It was a picture to see Hannah sitting calmly and unconcerned, like a 'swell' in a Rolls Royce."

Little wonder that Bill was said to have given her the rogue horses in his mobs because her riding ability, gentle skill and patience would win them over in the end. When Hannah was in her late teens tragedy stuck yet again; Bill was killed in a riding accident. Hannah sold up, keeping only a couple of riding horses and one to pack, and rode west. She would have been about seventeen years old.

Some time in 1889 she met a Victorian-born boundary rider, Tom Doyle, and in October that year they were married in the Charleville Church of England. Doyle, twenty-six, was a peculiar, jealous character. At the inquest into his suicide sixteen months after their marriage Hannah said he continually accused her of infidelity, saying that another man was the father of the child she was carrying.

She left him several times but each time he followed her and talked her into returning. Once he sprinkled strychnine on a piece of pudding and threatened to eat it if she did not return. Their child, a daughter, was born in Cunnamulla on 5 July 1890, during one of the couple's periods of separation. Of premature birth, Daisy died four days later .

When Hannah finally left Doyle for good the following January after more accusations and some physical abuse, she went to the Blackwater Hotel in Adavale. Doyle followed immediately but she refused his pleas. Three weeks later he returned and when he realised Hannah meant it this time he borrowed gun, powder and shot from the publican, saying he wanted to shoot some turkey next day. Instead, sitting under a tree outside the hotel, he turned the gun on himself. The local saddler found him with his shirt on fire, badly wounded but still alive. He told the saddler he had shot himself "on account of her". Later, as Hannah sat beside her dying husband, he told her: "It was all through you, Hannah." She was eighteen years old at the time. Having seen her father, stepfather, mother, brother and baby die, now she was being held responsible for the violent death of her husband. Her statement to the inquest into Doyle's suicide was taken in longhand by a visiting J.P. In her signature on the document "Hannah" is carefully written, as if through years of practice, but her married name, which she bore for just sixteen months, is oddly scrawled.

The signature closed the last official chapter in the life of Hannah Doyle, but it started the life and the legend of Red Jack. After the Adavale inquest in 1891 Hannah strapped her worldly possessions onto a packhorse and rode into the outback, where oblivion has swallowed up so many haunted souls. There is little doubt she worked on the far western runs, maybe even up to the Gulf, droving and doing stock work. One popular story has her dressing in black and keeping suitors away with her stockwhip.

She was already a mysterious local legend when she came riding out of the bush to wave down Durack's coach in 1898.

Several westerners, including Monica Terry up in the Hughenden district, recall meetings with old stockmen and drovers up to half a century ago who spoke of an exceptional horsewoman they had known or heard about in younger days. They all referred to her outstanding riding ability and her preference to work and travel alone. They were surely talking of Red Jack.

No doubt some of the scant legend about her is true, but the official facts recently uncovered are more mundane — Hannah had another daughter, Mary Doyle, several months after Doyle's suicide and later had two more children, a son George in 1893 and a daughter Ada in 1902. The father was not identified on the birth certificates.

She has a great-grandson, Frank Wieland, in Herberton. Frank told me his grandmother, who was adopted out soon after birth and had a particularly tough life, refused to speak of her mother, Red Jack, and that little was known of her life except for Mary Durack's poem. It is believed Hannah died of blood poisoning two days after Ada's birth. She is believed to be buried in Mareeba cemetery but neither her headstone nor a death certificate can be found.

"...any Great-coats... all the go in Bundah."

BOULIA

Three-Dog Night

Many's the Queensland drover who would have voted Boulia hawker Cliff Donohue to the highest office in the land, even unto the Lodge in Canberra, had they the opportunity back in the post-war years. For there was no sight in far western Queensland that warmed their hearts and bodies like that of Cliff driving his Dodge ute through the scrub with hobble chains, billy cans and quartpots ajangle as he bumped over broken ground into their camps.

But it wasn't grog he brought. The first rule in the hawker's handbook is: don't sell grog in a drover's camp because not only will you not be invited back by the boss drover, but the men will get hopelessly shickered on the rum and you won't sell a bloody thing . . . the pocket knives, mouth organs, hats, boots and all the paraphernalia so essential to a drover's day-to-day survival. No! Certainly not grog. What Cliff had that the drovers needed desperately were blankets and army greatcoats, and plenty of them.

You see, the droving season on that Northern Territory–Queensland stock route — which saw tens of thousands of bullocks walk from stations south of Darwin for fattening on the vast Channel Country runs — lasted roughly from May to August. It was simply too hot to push cattle thousands of kilometres in the summer. So when the drovers signed on for the job in the tropics they were hot, broke and travelling light in moleskins, the laughing-sided boot and cotton work shirts. Two and a half months later, with the cattle moving southeast over the Queensland border towards Boulia, the first civilisation since the drovers took delivery of the mob, they were flush with wages, having nowhere to spend even a lousy zac along the track. They were also bitterly cold in their summer clothes.

Back in Cliff's Boulia store, even today the kind of shop that has absolutely everything, Cliff monitored the movement of mobs on the road with the help of the bush telegraph. He often received telegraphed requests from droving camps to meet them somewhere along the stock route outside Boulia. Although there are still cattle camps operating with their plant horses today, back in the forties and fifties — before road transport took over — it was nothing to have three and four droving plants poking mobs past Boulia each week. Of course it was no good the hawker/storekeeper waiting until the drovers got to town because most likely they would stick their heads in at the pub first and not be seen again until they had just enough cash left to buy the barest essentials. So Cliff, as did all hawkers, met the drovers on the road anything up to forty kilometres out of town.

"Sometimes they'd almost knock me down begging for greatcoats and blankets," Cliff remembers. "They'd be shivering by day because they only had summer clothes, and at night they'd be shivering in their swags because they didn't have enough blankets." And it was no joke about drovers on the stock routes "nearer in" taking their dogs to bed for warmth.

"One time an old boss drover named Bert Crouch had his two sons working with him when I drove into their camp," said Cliff. "Bert bought about half a dozen slabs of chocolate besides his usual stores and some winter clothes. Anyway, we were sitting round the campfire after tea when the old man turned in early. A bit later his two boys decided to get into their swags too because it was pretty cold and they started calling their three dogs but couldn't find them. After a while they discovered they were in their father's swag.

"The young blokes kicked up a bit of a stink because they wanted a dog each to keep them warm. They were pleading with their old man: 'Come on, dad, give us a bloody dog, hey?' But the old man just said: 'Yes, well. I bought them some chocolates from Cliff, didn't I, and you didn't, did ya? So the bloody dogs are staying with me, see?' "

It really was a three-dog night. Cliff recalls those hawking days from the forties to the early seventies as the best of his life. "They were great blokes, the drovers, the salt of the earth. There was never a dull moment. Most of them are gone now because road trains took over long ago. But some are still around using stockhorses like in the old days. There's Johnny Stuart, the bloke Ted Egan wrote the song about, 'Johnny Stuart, Drover'. Johnny was through Boulia just the other day after a pretty hard time down Thargomindah way. They walked a mob of 1250 bullocks about 900 kilometres from Rocklands up near Camooweal down to Bulloo Downs but struck some rain a few days short of Bulloo.

"Their truck bogged and the motorbike they use to bring the horses on to camp ran out of petrol, but their stockhorses kept going. But with no truck to bring up their gear they spent the last three nights sleeping in their work clothes on the bare ground in the rain. They probably could have used some of my greatcoats like in the old days, but they delivered the mob safely anyway."

Cliff has taken some pretty strange orders from drovers on the track. One time he received a telegram, sent from a station along the way, asking him if he could get in a set of false teeth and it didn't matter what size or shape. But most telegrams usually only told him the size of the travelling mob and the station they were passing to let him know when they would be within striking distance of Cliff's rare old Dodge ute with its big wheels and high diff. It's retired now but still in a shed at the back of the store awaiting restoration — a real museum piece.

Hawkers like Cliff were always welcomed by the drovers as much for their news and gossip as their goods. "They wanted to know what had been going on in the world," Cliff recalled. "Not just world news but what was going on locally, who married who, that sort of gossip. They were starved for news."

How different it is today. Recently I received a call from an old showman, Brian Gill, who was ringing from his car phone in the desert near the West Australian–Northern Territory border where he was taking his buck-jump show to isolated Aboriginal communities. That morning he'd been watching a Sydney show on his portable TV which featured another old trouper claiming to be the last of the fair dinkum travelling showmen. Gill called me to light-heartedly have a go at the bloke on TV whom he knew from the old days. "What the bloody hell's he think I'm doing out here in the desert with my travelling show, having a holiday?" Brian asked me.

But there were no car phones or television in the outback in the droving days. When Cliff Donohue drove his ute into camp it was like two months of newspapers arriving at once.

Probably the only thing he didn't have in common with his drover mates was their general acceptance of almost anything the camp cook served up. By his own admission Cliff is pretty particular about hygiene and the way his food is prepared. So he wasn't real keen on the fare served up years ago at one droving camp.

"The boss drover wasn't what you'd call hygienic," Cliff recalled. "In fact he was a bit on the nose and they reckon the only time he had a bath was when he had to swim his horse across a flooded creek every so often. So I was a bit surprised when he told me he'd have to sack his cook. He reckoned the cook was the dirtiest bugger he'd ever seen. He must have been real crook."

If you're ever out Boulia way you should take a look in Donohue's store. If he doesn't stock it then you won't need it outback, whatever it is.

"unity's shin plasters . . ."

WINDORAH

Suffering Shin Plasters!

If my old man had his way about sixty-five years ago I'd be a filthy rich cattle baron today, lord of all I surveyed and calling no man my master — except for a daily grovel to my esteemed bank manager, of course. Instead, my mum won the argument and took dad off the land forever, ending up in a country pub for better or worse.

Unfortunately it was nothing like the good old country pub days of earlier this century when western Queensland publicans actually printed their own flimsy currency, handing it out as change for large cheques and knowing it would often crumble to dust before it could be cashed against the publican's account at some distant bank. Most pubs and businesses in towns without banks, places like Windorah and Boulia, had their own paper notes printed, which were widely traded throughout the west as legal tender. Notes ranged from five shillings to five pounds, and styles varied from the plain-looking IOUs of tiny Hamilton Hotel in the wilderness outside Boulia, to grandly scrolled and elaborately printed notes from Windorah's Western Star Hotel, in pounds sterling, no less.

These notes were traded on goods and services but could only be cashed for real money at the bank designated thereon, usually several hundred miles away. A primary purpose was to cash shearers' cheques, because few pubs kept enough hard cash to cope with the huge cheques which crossed the bar when mobs of thirsty shearers hit town after a shed cut out.

There is a lovely story about a city traveller's chance meeting with Windorah publican Mrs Unity McPhellamy in 1917 in a back room of the Western Star. He had wandered out the back looking for service because the bar was empty. There he found Unity personally signing hundreds of her fancy notes in preparation for that night's rip-roaring trading: a big shed down the Cooper was due to cut out that afternoon. While she was explaining the private currency to the stranger, the yardman popped in and, nodding to the notes, asked Mrs McPhellamy: "Will I give 'em the treatment, missus?"

"No," she explained. "This is a good lot of blokes coming tonight and they'll be back again next shearing season."

The traveller later discovered the "treatment" was a ten minute stint in a very hot oven which made the notes dry, brittle and unable to stand a bit of manhandling before crumbling to dust. Even without the "treatment", private notes were nowhere near as robust as real money and many simply disintegrated from overuse and sweat and were never cashed in, leaving the publican's account so much the better. But drinkers were nothing if not resourceful and the smart ones used to carry their private notes plastered flat to the skin around their shins, hence the notes became widely known as "shin plaster".

Ah! Such a fate may have befallen me had I been born into a pub a hundred years ago. The last of the "shin plasters" was traded in Boulia around 1942 and by that time my parents had moved from a western pub to one at Yeppoon by the sea, a long way from circumstances in which I may have learned to make a fortune pushing rotgut grog and self-destructing money. Not that I didn't learn a few tricks from an early life in a pub; a real education it was, and the first lesson was to be pleasant to everyone but trust no one.

So it was with great interest that Hugh Sawrey and I listened as Boulia publican, John Tully, related the sad but amazing tale of a young man who passed through last Christmas. "You wouldn't read about this," Tully started out, but I told him not to bet on it. The young bloke

hitched into town with a school teacher who was on his
way from the Kimberleys in far north western Australia
to spend Christmas in Melbourne with his dear old mum.
He stood the school teacher food, grog and overnight
accommodation and saw him on his way next day, deciding to stay on in Boulia to look for an old friend.

A couple of days later he had run up a substantial bill
but Tully didn't worry because they trust people out that
way. However, on the morning of the third day not only
was the lodger gone, but so was Tully's truck and all his
and his mates' camping and brumby catching equipment,
including a motorbike, generator and refrigerator, total
value around $10,000.

For the next couple of days Tully spent an awful lot of
time telling his customers what he'd do if that young bloke
and the teacher ever came back and it wasn't a pretty tale.
I know, because he told us a couple of times, with those
gnarled bushman's hands twisting in opposite directions
like they were breaking someone's neck. Christmas came
and went and just into the new year who should walk into
the pub for a beer but the school teacher returning to the
Kimberleys after Christmas in Melbourne.

The wronged publican couldn't believe his eyes and
was on the wrong side of the bar in a flash, preparing to
flatten the startled school teacher after giving him an
earful of abuse first. When the fuss died down and the
teacher was able to get a word in edgeways he explained
that he didn't know what the publican was talking about
because he only picked up the young bloke west of Boulia
in the Northern Territory and hadn't seen him before. But
he had some other surprising news.

By an amazing coincidence a couple of hours earlier
east of Boulia he picked up the same bloke hitching back
to the Territory. The young bloke had been very surprised
to see him and became a little agitated when the teacher
insisted on stopping at the Boulia pub to shout him a beer
for his generosity a few weeks earlier. The young bloke
said he didn't want to stop at the hotel because the
publican was a raving lunatic and would probably try to

punch them — which appeared to be the case when the teacher walked into the bar just a few minutes earlier.

The teacher let the young bloke out just down the road and drove on to the pub looking for a cold beer when the world just about caved in on him. Not for long, though, because the wild-eyed publican was out the pub door like a shot and down the road looking for the young bloke who robbed him of $10,000. But the conman had taken to the scrub despite searing heat. He was nabbed next day, close to perishing. Fortunately the police grabbed him first and would not listen to the publican's pleas to have a few quiet moments alone with him.

To cut a long story short the conman had driven Tully's ute to Townsville where he said some thieving scoundrels pilfered the stolen gear from the back, then dumped the vehicle. He spent Christmas day with a long-lost uncle, asked for a loan of the family car to drive to the shop for some smokes and kept right on driving. He was heading back to the Territory when his uncle's car ran out of petrol 20 kilometres east of Boulia, where he again flagged down the teacher.

There was no record of how many other cars or how much property he had stolen on his Christmas holidays in Queensland. He got three months jail but John Tully didn't get a cent for his lost $10,000 in stolen goods or food, grog and accommodation bill.

I didn't ask him, but I reckon John Tully wouldn't mind returning to the old days when a western publican could make enough profit out of a handful of suitably treated "shin plasters" to cover losses inflicted by the occasional travelling conman.

"The Fighting Padré"

OUTER BARCOO

A Round with the Punching Padre

Beyond the Outer Barcoo where churches are few and men of religion are absolutely scanty, Father Laurie Whiting tends a ragged flock which would have inspired the devil in Banjo Paterson. After seven years as Catholic priest to parishioners scattered over thousands of square kilometres around Winton, nothing surprises Fr Whiting — which is just as well. Not even the time, several years ago, when the isolated miners of harsh, dry Opalton invited him down to celebrate a special pre-festive season Mass at which they would reflect on distant loved ones, many of whom would experience a white Christmas in far-off Europe.

The date was set for late one Saturday afternoon, allowing Fr Whiting time to say regular morning Mass in Winton, roll his swag, pick up a lump of steak for the post-Mass barbecue, and drive the 130 bumpy kilometres south to the mining shanty town. But ere Fr Whiting had finished saying Mass in Winton, the Devil himself had visited Opalton in the form of several Sydney opal buyers, who snapped up everything on offer at record prices.

"They were unexpectedly high prices, so the miners had been celebrating long before I arrived," Fr Whiting recalled.

By the time he set up the altar on a forty-four gallon drum, the sun was sinking slowly in the west and his congregation's spirits were absolutely soaring, stumbling as they were into that makeshift holy place clutching stubbies as well as prayer books. Some were so uplifted they forgot where they were, pulled out the makings and lit up, only to be howled down by more sober worshippers.

Wisely reading the mood of the congregation, Fr Whiting decided to substitute the Mass with a more concise prayer and hymn service. Even so he recalled being inspired by the beautiful sunset and waxing eloquent on the wonders of nature and God until one lost soul stood up to declare himself rowdily against police, politics and religion. No one minded the first two objections but the third provoked several to drag him a discreet distance into the scrub for counselling. Fr Whiting recalled the objector returning to his makeshift pew "suitably chastened" and this strange congregation of about fifty happy, ragged souls got on with their hymn singing and reflection on the folks they'd left far away.

The fun continued at the post-service barbecue where several other worshippers had to be counselled, one for threatening to blow the speakers out of a neighbour's car radio because it was playing stirring martial music. Things may have become more lively but Fr Whiting didn't stick around, deciding things were already "too willing too early". He jumped in his 4WD and put a few miles between himself and his congregation before unrolling his swag by the track.

Such is life for a bush cleric in the jet age, but the more things change the more they remain the same. I give you the case of an incredible young Englishman, Brother Fred Hulton Sams of the Anglican Bush Brotherhood. He took some beating, physically as well as spiritually. He was dubbed the Fighting Parson because, after delivering his sermon, Bro. Hulton Sams would invite members of his congregation to step outside for a round or two in the churchyard. He was an above average grass fighter and always carried two pairs of boxing gloves over his saddle on his religious rounds through some of the west's toughest territory.

Back then survival was the name of the game, even on a religious round, and one time, riding alone from Bedourie to Boulia, Bro. Hulton Sams almost perished when his horses cleared out overnight. Looking for them next day he became hopelessly lost. Some time later, when Sams was exhausted and out of water, fate took a hand. Two youngsters, the sons of an isolated bore driller, were looking for their father's horses when they crossed Bro. Hulton Sams's tracks, followed them, and the parson lived to fight another day.

Although he fought many rough and tumble ringers from his congregations before the First World War, his contests with a bruising bush champion, Big Will Watson of Currawilla, were legendary around far western cattle camps for many years after our hero's death in action in France. At the outbreak of war in 1914 Bro. Hulton Sams returned to England to enlist in the Duke of Cornwall's Light Infantry and received a commission as lieutenant.

A letter to his sister from the battalion adjutant told the story of his death: "I talked to your brother several times. He was magnificent and very cheerful. His last words to me were: 'Well, old boy, this is a bit thick but we'll see it through, never fear.' . . . at about 10 a.m. your brother crawled away to get any water for his men, many of whom were wounded and very thirsty. He was hit by a piece of shell and killed instantly. He died doing a thing which makes us feel proud to have known him. He was a fine officer, a fine friend and was worshipped by his men."

Another Bush Brother from the same vast western parish was to die at the hands of a different enemy in another war. Before the Second World War Bro. Vivian Redlich was a very welcome visitor in the back country, as much for his mechanical as his spiritual skills. Consequently he spent more time hovering over conked-out station engines than he did over makeshift pulpits.

In the late thirties he volunteered for missionary work in Papua and was later caught up in the Japanese invasion. When the Japanese landed he and two Australian female missionaries joined a small party of Europeans in the jungle, relying on villagers for food and concealment as they fled. Unfortunately a village leader named Esega turned them over to the Japanese. In August 1942 the party of nine, including a six-year-old boy, were executed on a beach at Buna, each one beheaded by the same bloodthirsty officer. After the war the villager was hung for betraying the Europeans.

Bush clergy beyond the Outer Barcoo saw some fine philosophers; Winton's Catholic priest from 1903 to 1911, Father John Fagen, was a good example. Asked once by a priggish brother minister what were the moral values of the disgusting social and sporting gatherings which are held all too infrequently in the bush, Fr Fagen replied: "One good social gathering is worth twenty of your sermons. They are simply putting into practice the virtues we preach from the pulpit . . . virtues of hospitality, charity and gratitude."

And what did the hardy old westerner think of holy men in the bush? Listen to Winton pioneer, bullocky and politician, W.H. Corfield, who summed it up beautifully when he wrote at the turn of the century. "I cannot help thinking that politics are the bane of the west. It is singularly free from religious rancour or animosity. The religious belief of the other man, or if he has any at all, concerns no one. So long as a clergyman does not hold that playing cricket or football on Sunday is wrong, even if he is not popular, he is at all times respected." My oath!

The Far North

CAPE YORK

Nursing the Baby North

I would like a quid for every person who asked the state of the road and the type of vehicle best suited for the trip up Cape York Peninsula. Such questions always got the same piece of advice — don't attempt it in the family sedan and certainly try to do it in a four-wheel-drive, preferably with a winch.

You could do it in a conventional vehicle with lots of care in a good season but there's a good chance you will wreck the car long before you reach the tip of the Cape. They don't build conventional sedans tough enough for those roads. Then again, you might not need to switch your vehicle into 4WD more than once or twice in the entire trip, but when you have to, well, there's just no other way.

It comes as a great surprise to learn that more than sixty years ago, when the horse was still king of the far north and roads were little more than wallaby pads, locals and adventurers were driving those crazy old rag-hood, wire-wheeled roadsters through the scrub. More remarkable is the fact that the first car to make the trip up Cape York Peninsula to the Tip, from Sydney as a matter of fact, was an Austin Seven — a "Baby Austin" they were dubbed — back in 1928. A bloke named Hector McQuarrie was the driver and he had to be a mad Pom because the tiny Austin flew a Union Jack from its radiator cap.

If you want a mental picture of the Baby Austin think of one of those big old cane prams, take away the handle, attach tiny headlights and that's it. They were frail, motorised billycarts that looked like they would fall to bits at the first pothole. But what remarkable cars they were and what remarkable drivers to nurse them thousands of kilometres through trackless northern isolation.

Sixty-three years on, with formed dirt roads, road-houses, pubs and hundreds of fellow travellers kicking up dust, the trip to the Tip is still one of Australia's last big adventures. Hugh Sawrey and I covered more than 4000 kilometres meandering up and back from Towns-ville in Hugh's Landcruiser ute, towing a trailer we didn't need. That's the rig parked under the mango trees outside the Quinkin Pub at Laura in Hugh's sketch.

Although most travel in air-conditioned 4WD comfort, motorbikes are extremely popular, particularly with young Japanese adventurers — kamikazes, locals call them. We discovered one young Jap rider broken down in the middle of nowhere after hitting a small creek at a thousand kilometres a minute. Two hired 4WDs had pulled over to help him, one driven by a Pom tourist and the other by a German. It was an interesting roadside conversation with each party restricted to his native tongue.

One day in an isolated far northern pub, Hugh and I were yarning with a slow-talking local when he recalled one of the highlights of his bush life. A couple of years ago, a kamikaze and his girlfriend came buzzing up the Cape, he on a powerful machine and she on a two-stroke that was shaking her to bits. She was never going to make it to the Tip on that machine so she decided to camp at the pub and wait for the boyfriend's return. One night she got a little tipsy and confessed in broken English she hadn't come to Australia to ride up Cape York so much as to marry an Aussie and settle here.

Our friend telling us the yarn took a sip of beer and there was a long silence as he stared across the dusty road to where a rather large woman was screeching like a mob of cockatoos at a half dozen snot-nosed brats.

"That's me missus," he said in a soft voice that seemed

to come from a distant horizon. "Sometimes I reckon I should have bought a motorbike and cleared off with that little Jap sheila."

CHARLOTTE ST
COOKTOWN
"JACKEY-JACKEY" STORE
IN FOREGROUND.   SAWREY '91

COOKTOWN

Temptation in the Tropics

It would be extremely hard to find an Australian town with a past like Cooktown's, even considering the wide gap between historical fact and wild fiction about the rip-roaring northern port. Bold and brassy, Cooktown sprang from the mangrove-lined south bank of the Endeavour River after gold was discovered on the Palmer River in 1873. Over the next decade Cooktown was the centre of the universe for tens of thousands of wild-eyed prospectors and fewer wild, wild women. Population estimates range from 2500 to 60,000, but local historians say the figure was more like 4000 at its peak between 1874 and 1885, with anything up to 35,000 men on the Palmer diggings and surrounding goldfields at any one time.

Nearing the end of the first year of the rush there were 94 licensed pubs and many illegal shanties in Cooktown. The brothel count ranged from 60 to 160, though no one knows for sure — they didn't need licences back then. A pioneering journalist writing from Cooktown for a southern newspaper in March 1874, just five months after the town was born, observed in one of his rambling accounts of local triumphs and tragedies: "I see there are two or three dance-houses here and several women. I thought that it would be a rare thing to see a woman here."

Two or three dance-houses and several women? Who did he think he was kidding? Here's a reporter sitting in the middle of a steamy boom town and he can't decide if there are two or three dance-houses or count the number of women in the middle of a tropical wilderness, I ask ya? Maybe he had a jealous wife back home and didn't want to make his tough assignment in the balmy tropics look too good. (That's never happened to me, though. It's always tough.)

There is little doubt that, soon after, Cooktown became as wild and woolly a frontier town as Australia has seen. By the end of 1874 there were ninety-plus pubs and many unlicensed sly grogers, scores of brothels, gambling and opium dens, twenty eating houses, six butchers, twelve large stores, bakers, chemists, doctors, tent-makers, blacksmiths, even six hairdressers. There were three local newspapers, the *Herald* and the *Courier* and, for a few months, a Chinese language newspaper. God was also there, but only just. Cooktown had just two churches, Catholic and Anglican.

You could get just about anything you needed there in the seventies and eighties last century, but it came at a very high price. Transport costs and exploitation saw to that. Gold was the favoured currency with all businesses, and the lucky miners who had it threw it around like confetti, because there was always plenty more back on the Palmer — the River of Gold, they called it.

Not all the feverish miners struck it rich. For although the goldfield yielded 1.35 million ounces of gold, as well as what was smuggled out by Chinese overlords, the majority of miners came down from the Palmer as sadder but wiser men, many without the price of a feed, let alone the price of a boat trip back home.

Fittingly Cooktown today has a very bright future in tourism, not only for the nostalgic appeal of its golden frontier days, but for its close links with Captain James Cook who proclaimed "the whole eastern coast" as New South Wales, the property of King George III, from Cooktown's muddy shores. If you went there and didn't know that Captain James Cook spent his longest time on Australian soil slap bang in the middle of town, then you would soon be reminded of it. Cooktown is all about Cook, from his memorial on the Endeavour River, which he named after his ship, to the wonderful museum in the century-old former convent, St Mary's.

Go to Cooktown as Hugh Sawrey and I did in the weeks leading up to the 16 June anniversary of the badly-holed *Endeavour* arriving in the river for repairs and most likely you will see an assorted bunch of locals rehearsing that landing of 1770. We saw them in thongs and shorts, rowing longboats, and presenting replica muskets — like Brown's cows coming in for milking. They were having a ball, as a matter of fact, and looking forward to a few stubbies sitting in the autumn sun after rehearsals.

The narrator, local school teacher Ross Mackay, assured us all would go like a well-oiled machine on anniversary day. "On the day you'd swear they'd just marched in from Buckingham Palace," he said. It was hard to imagine as they marched around the historic spot where Cook camped while extensive repairs were made to his ship.

Thereabouts Cook's men had their first real encounter with Aborigines, and his botanist, the young swell Joseph Banks, his first real contact with the continent's plants and wildlife. Most of his 180 observations of new plants and animals were made there. The foundations were also laid for our feral pig problem when some of the *Endeavour*'s porkers escaped. What must the common sailors have thought of filthy rich young Banks who had paid 10,000 pounds sterling to make the voyage of discovery, bringing with him two Negro servants, two greyhounds and five helpers? What must the local Aborigines have thought on 4 August 1770 when they saw the *Endeavour* finally disappear over the eastern horizon, no doubt wishing the ship and Cook good bloody riddance?

Still, they had another hundred-odd years of isolation left before the lure of Palmer River gold brought the rush that changed their lives forever.

COOKTOWN

Three Hearty Cheers for the Captain

History books mostly overlook the human drama of great events, and it is often reflected in anniversaries like Australia Day. Re-enactments feature pompous people in fancy dress raising flags and reading proclamations, not the drama of past daily life. Now I know we are not feting Captain James Cook's epic voyage on our national holiday, but anyone who likes Australia the way it is should be grateful for the dramatic events that kept him from sinking forever off the Queensland coast before he could tell England of the great south land.

Had Cook, his crew and his barque sunk on Endeavour Reef on 10 June 1770, as it certainly might have, what would have been this country's fate — its creed, its language, its colour and its customs — today? Indeed what would it have been called? And what of our fate? I don't know about you, but I can see myself sitting on a one-hectare potato farm in Ireland with 20,000 close relatives trying to establish which square centimetre belonged to me and my brood.

Instead, because of Cook's luck, I celebrated Australia Day reading extracts from his journal and thanking my lucky stars that his bones and those of the *Endeavour* are not lying unheralded on the Great Barrier Reef. Cook and his men actually thought they were bound for Davy Jones's locker when the full extent of their grounding on the reef became evident some hours after the impact at eleven p.m. They jettisoned 50 tons of cargo, including six cannon, and put out five anchors trying to winch themselves off the reef, to no avail. But let Captain Cook tell you (he was on the quarter-deck at the time):

> During all this time she continued to beat with great violence against the rock, so that it was with utmost difficulty that we kept upon our legs; and to complete the scene of distress we saw by the light of the moon the sheathing boards from the bottom of the vessel floating away all round her, and at last her false keel, so that every moment was making way for the sea to rush in which was to swallow us up.

The thoughts of godless old tars vainly striving at the pumps to keep pace with the incoming water suddenly turned to the hereafter and they sought heavenly favours, as Cook observed: ". . . the men were so far imprest with a sense of their situation that not an oath was heard among them, the habit of profaneness, however strong, being instantly subdued by the dread of incurring guilt when death seemed so near."

Worse news was to follow at daylight when, with the barque still pounding on the reef and pumps unable to keep pace, they realised they were about 40 kilometres from land and Cook speculated on the chance of survival if the ship's company was forced into the longboats: "We well knew our boats were not capable of carrying us all on shore and that when the dreadful crisis should arrive...a contest for preference would probably ensue that would increase the horrors even of shipwreck and terminate in the destruction of us all by the hands of each other."

Then came Cook's first stroke of luck. The wind and sea, which had been pounding the *Endeavour* on the reef throughout the night and morning, eased. The barque's four pumps, at this stage manned by exhausted men who could only give a few minutes' effort before collapsing on deck, barely kept pace with the leaks. Cook had no doubt that the dramatic change to a dead-calm ocean saved their lives.

Temporary repairs were urgently needed to get the ship to safe anchorage (later found where Cooktown now stands). Here again Cook was in luck because one of his midshipmen had been in similar circumstances in America, when a crippled ship was saved by a system known as "fothering". Cook had not heard of it but gave it a go. It involved stitching wool and rope fibre on to a spare sail; and ". . . over this he spread the dung of our sheep and other filth", and hauled the sail and mixture down the hull and over the holes where water pressure held it fast. It worked and Cook sailed cautiously for the mainland.

Twelve days later, when the barque was beached in the Endeavour River and the tide went out, Cook for the first time fully appreciated his extreme good fortune, for low water revealed a huge chunk of coral still plugging the major hole in the hull. Eight pumps manned by fit men, let alone the four aboard the *Endeavour*, would not have saved his ship had it not been for the coral, Cook wrote in his journal.

Of course Cook's troubles were far from over, what with a couple of dirty big holes to repair and the nearest shipyards 19,000 kilometres away. But his men were a self-sufficient lot, making their own bolts and nails and cutting new timber, and six weeks later they were on their way, and the great south land came under British rule.

I'm glad he made it because I wouldn't fancy scratching a living out of a few square centimetres of the Olde Sod. For the record, Cook's six cannon and one anchor were recovered from Endeavour Reef in 1969. One cannon and the anchor are in Cooktown Museum, others are in England, the United States, New Zealand and New South Wales.

"MRS. WATSON ... THE ESCAPE FROM LIZARD ISLAND"

LIZARD ISLAND

Escape to Nowhere

The woman sweeping the wide veranda outside our rooms in Cooktown looked mighty like someone with something on her mind. You blokes are from the city newspaper, aren't ya? she suddenly asked of Hugh and myself between impatient strokes of her broom. Right! Well, why don't you do something about getting Mrs Watson's tank back up here where it belongs! She commanded this with the directness you expect from a woman of the wilderness.

The absence of Mrs Watson's tank is a sore point in Cooktown. She and her three month old boy Ferrier are buried there, a grand memorial to her stands in the main street, and locals believe the 1.2 metre-square, iron ship's tank in which she made her epic, tragic escape from Aboriginal attack on Lizard Island should be based there too. In fact Mrs Watson's memory stands almost as tall as that of Captain James Cook and it is impossible to visit Cooktown without hearing about her life which ended abruptly back in 1881.

Hers is one of the few recorded stories of northern women in a man's untamed land and its survival is due only to the high drama surrounding her death, which she recorded stoically in a diary. Yet her life, without the drama of her death, was worthy of a small place in north Queensland's history, as were the lives of so many women standing silently, often alone, behind history's heroes.

Mrs Watson was a twenty-one-year-old school teacher

who gave up the comfort of Cooktown in the 1881 goldrush days to live in a lonely hut on Lizard Island with her new husband Robert Watson, a bêche-de-mer fisherman. When their first child was only three months old Watson and his partner sailed off to establish a fishing station about 300 kilometres away, leaving only Mrs Watson and their two Chinese workers on the island, almost 100 kilometres away from the nearest civilisation, at Cooktown. And there was no boat.

Soon after Watson left in September 1881, a group of mainland Aborigines paddled dug-out canoes many kilometres across open ocean to Lizard. Their arrival utterly surprised Mrs Watson, but if you have visited Lizard Island, which has one of the most beautiful sandy bays in Queensland, you would realise it was a traditional seafood feasting place long before Captain Cook stepped ashore. Mrs Watson began recording events in her diary soon after seeing smoke from campfires on 27 September.

Over the next few days one of the Chinese was killed and the other speared seven times. On 2 October Mrs Watson loaded her badly wounded servant Ah Sam, her baby and some provisions into the ship's tank, which had been used to boil bêche-de-mer, and paddled out to sea. The last diary entry, on October 11, read: "Nearly dead with thirst."

On 19 January 1882 the bodies of Mrs Watson and her baby were found in the tank on No. 5 Horwick Island. Ah Sam's body was found nearby. They had somehow paddled seventy kilometres through open sea in what was little more than a boiling pot.

Today the tank is a major attraction at Townsville's Tropical Queensland Museum, and the museum doesn't want to part with it. That's a battle for the women of Cooktown and it could be an epic tale in itself.

Another epic tale of female endurance in north Queensland can be found in the amazing story of Torres Strait shipwreck survivor Barbara Thompson back in 1844. Start with the account in a recent book, *The Savage Frontier* by Rodney Liddell, which was given to me at Red

Island Point on the tip of Cape York. In 1843, aged fifteen, Barbara eloped from Sydney with the skipper of a twelve-tonne cutter and was married soon after in Moreton Bay. On an old tar's word they sailed for Torres Strait, chasing shipwreck booty, and were shipwrecked themselves near Thursday Island — but not before stranding the old tar on a sandbank to drown for telling lies about the booty.

Barbara Thompson was clinging to life on the wreck, a lone survivor in headhunting territory 1600 kilometres from civilisation, when a war canoe paddled up. Far from killing her, the warriors took her to Prince of Wales Island where their chief welcomed her as the spirit of his daughter Giom, who had died only weeks before. It was not unusual for Aborigines and Islanders to look on whites as spirits returned from the dead, and luckily Barbara Thompson bore a resemblance to the chief's daughter.

For the next five years she lived a nightmare tribal existence, jealously guarded at all times to prevent escape. She even received a proposal from a desperate escaped convict known as Wini who had set himself up as chief of Badu Island, and turned his warriors into a bunch of murderers who killed castaways and made frequent unprovoked raids on more peaceful island tribes.

Barbara Thompson's almost unbelievable five-year drama ended on 16 October 1849, when she was rescued by government ships charting a safe passage through the strait. It was some time before she could make herself understood because she had almost forgotten English, but she settled back in Sydney, married again, and died aged eighty-four, in 1912.

The music-lovers

Silent Night, Unholy Night

Back in 1963 they called Hugh Sawrey "Banjo Paterson with a paint brush" because of a wandering life in which he painted murals from the poet's works on bush pub walls for his bed, a feed and a beer or two. And with typical modesty, I claim credit for the dubbing in a feature I wrote on Sawrey when he was paying his way at the long gone Royal Hotel opposite the Brisbane GPO, painting the walls for his keep.

At the time I didn't know how appropriate it was. Only on our trip up Cape York did I realise how often the painter quoted the bard after which he was nicknamed, Banjo Patterson. And not only to me, but to passing cattle, horses, kookaburras, anything that moved. It started our first night on the road, with Hugh reciting my favourite, "The Story of Mongrel Grey", sitting on his swag on an incredibly starry night on a back-road camp that would have inspired the Banjo himself.

This is the story stockman told
On the cattle-camp, when the stars were bright;
The moon rose up like a globe of gold
And flooded the plains with her mellow light.
We watched the cattle till dawn of day
And he told me the story of Mongrel Grey.

Ah, yes! It was my favourite textbook work at school. I wonder do they still teach Paterson, Lawson and Boake as well as Shakespeare? A great pity if they don't.

It was a crisp, silent night. We finished our tea and

crawled into our swags and for the short space it took to start snoring I wondered how anyone, even the Banjo, could describe in written words such pristine stillness, such majestic isolation. There really is nothing to match the stillness of an outback night.

Peace reigned for an estimated two hours, then a utility moved into the deserted camp and parked about fifty metres away, its motor totally drowned out by a radio at full blast and sounding like a phantom ice-cream van riding with the ghost herd in the sky. In the clear, starlit night two figures emerged, unrolled their swags and were soon fast asleep with the radio still going full blast and both cabin doors wide open. Screeching disco music played between talk-back sessions in which a guru with a deep voice listened to the ravings of insomniacs, then solved their life's disasters in a trice.

The short story is that the radio raged on until four in the morning when the camp manager, nagged by his missus, as she told me next morning, jumped out of bed, got dressed (I know not why), and stormed across an open paddock to switch the radio off. During the night I had thought of being so brave, but I did something similar in the dead of night many years ago and ended up with my hand down a bull terrier's throat while his mate started gnawing away at the other end.

Next morning the camp manager's missus apologised for the loud radio, but we said not to worry because they were just a couple of stumbling drunks who went to sleep and forgot the radio. Not so, said the missus. They were railway workers from down the road who had had little to drink but who were just so used to loud radios, videos and television all day and all night back at the railway camp that they became immune to noise. With them, noise didn't even register until it was switched off and they noticed it missing. Silence deafened them, she said.

"Silence gives them headaches," she said. "Noise is like a tranquilliser. They eat with it, work with it and sleep with it back at the camp. I don't know where it will all end."

This made me wonder if we have not already bred a race of Australians who not only are dead to what this great country has to offer but who crave loud noise like a drug. Amazingly, the noise freaks who shattered, and no doubt are still shattering, the great Australian outback night were not youngsters but greybeards, probably the first greybearded products of the video age.

Alas, it soon became obvious on our trip that the Aussie bush has joined the city and officially passed from a timeless, peaceful land headlong into the video age where the ability to entertain oneself without buttons to push or levers to pull is just about dead — certainly with the average Aussies of the coming generation. As you wander further through the isolation of Queensland, through once quaint little bush towns not significant enough to be marked on the map, you get a fair idea what is happening to our ability to entertain ourselves or cope with the sounds of silence. Almost without exception, the smallest general store has more videotapes than loaves of bread, and at least one video game machine.

Videotapes line the most convenient shelves like small country libraries of bygone years; but unfortunately as the video age spreads, so the age of books retreats. As Sawrey remarked one sundown in historic Croydon, the gateway to the Gulf, small towns don't have the same feel they did just a few short years ago before TV and especially before video.

"Not so long ago this time of day you'd see a few ringers squatting around the place smoking and yarning or at least see a few kids out playing, but look at this," he said glancing around the deserted town. But from inside the homes came the flickering coloured lights of TV and video; outside, the town's giant satellite dish silently invoked plastic images from outer space like some primitive's cargo cult — only today the video gods really listen and rain down their useless cargo.

What Banjo Paterson would have said standing with us there in the Croydon sunset I can only imagine. I somehow fancy the Banjo wouldn't have had a lot of time for the video age. Sawrey doesn't, nor do I. But we'd have plenty of time for an Aussie system that switched off videos long enough to give Paterson, Lawson and friends — a fair dinkum Australia — a bit more of a go than it's getting today.

"Camp-oven and Billy-can"

"THE FOSSICKER"
PALMER RIVER
CAPE YORK PENINSULA
SAWREY 91

LYND RIVER

Struck by Gold Fever

You don't need to apologise to anyone for pulling your rocking boots on when Queensland wins against the odds, as the mighty Maroons did in the first State of Origin match for 1991. I remember it well because I heard the ABC's description in most unusual circumstances: all alone under the stars camped beside the Lynd River, slap bang in the middle of Cape York Peninsula. Sure, Hugh was with me but he was in his swag snoring his head off soon after kick-off. If they'd played the game on horseback he would have been yelling his head off with me, but men running around the paddock on foot don't interest him.

So there was I, listening to Big Artie tell it like it was, while having an occasional nip of rum on medical advice because up in the tropics even little things like crocodile bites can become infected if you don't take your medicine. Well, you probably won't believe this, but celebrating an Origin victory alone in the middle of the wilderness produces exactly the same result as celebrating victory with 35,000 other fans at Lang Park. Thus next day I was standing knee-deep in the Lynd just after dawn trying to drive out the evil spirits by dousing my head in cold river water.

Vision was almost fully restored as the first shafts of sunlight flashed over those still, clear waters. I studied my feet in the river-bed sand and was pleasantly relieved -- they were still at the end of my legs. I wriggled my toes;

all present and correct in that distant outpost. Just then I was struck by a lightning bolt. For between my toes, glittering yellow in the river sand was —

"Gold!" I was yelling at the top of my lungs, clawing up the steep bank, eyes bugging with the fever. "Hughie. It's gold. Tons of it down there in the sand. Gold, I tell you! We're rich. Get the pans out quick. We're filthy rich!"

Back at camp sitting on his swag Sawrey had a smile a mile wide. "It's iron pyrites, mate," he said. "Fool's gold. You're not the first to fall for it and you won't be the last."

So I won't. But it gave me a rare insight into what drove some men to cheat, rob and kill, to face outrageous odds against the wilderness, starvation, drowning, spear, crocodile, thirst and disease: the lust for gold. It was a very exciting moment or two, the climb up that bank, because I was rich beyond the dreams of avarice and knew that no one, not Bob Hawke, not the taxman, not even the editor, could reach me now. I was untouchable and if I'd had access to a public telephone I'd be out of a job right now.

For a fleeting moment I felt genuine gold fever and can begin to understand what all the fuss was about back in 1873 when 35,000 men began the rush to that river of gold, the Palmer, less than 100 kilometres from my discovery that post-Origin dawn. Many similarly afflicted men were murdered, drowned, or died of disease — some were even cooked and eaten. Some starved to death, their pockets stuffed with gold. There is no official death toll from the Palmer rush, either of white, yellow or black. But unmarked graves are spread far and wide around the Palmer district and up the brutal, deadly track from Cooktown, the port established specifically to open up the goldfields.

Death and privation notwithstanding, feverish men kept coming from overseas and from the south, by foot, horse, and wagon; by overcrowded steamers and sailing ships, and even small open boats all the way from Brisbane. Many were ill-prepared new chums completely ignorant of the harsh conditions ahead. The Chinese who flocked to the Palmer, and there were an estimated 20,000 on the field at one time, toiled until every speck was gathered before they moved on. This led to outbreaks of violence and racism, with white miners upset that the hard-working Chinese were robbing them of their back-stop, the gold dust they were too lazy or too greedy to work for when they were originally on the claims.

The Chinese were also on the receiving end from local Aborigines, some tribes being described as giant in stat-ure and very hostile in defence of their territory. They also allegedly practised cannibalism. Contemporary reports had them hanging Chinese by their pigtails in trees like meat in a butcher shop, awaiting future consumption. There are also accounts of tribesmen breaking miners' legs to prevent them escaping the pot. But it is highly unlikely that the violent deaths of white and yellow miners equalled more than a small proportion of the slaughter of local tribesmen. Aborigines were shot out of hand.

Add all this man-made violence to the natural dangers of the rugged north land, even today, and you have a pretty fair idea of what gold fever can do to you. It's a very powerful emotion, even experienced for just a fleeting moment. But learn the rules and play it safe: find out what real gold looks like before you tell the boss what he can do with his job.

SAWREY '91

"Cape York Cathedrals"

CAPE YORK

Ant Hill Cathedral

One night in the mid-fidties, a blinding flash of youthful exuberance enveloped me unexpectedly and I leapt into a tempestuous fandango in my mother-in-law's lounge room. It was a memorable moment in a young life for, on the first fiery stamp of my right foot, with arms gracefully raised and clacking imaginary castanets, I began to disappear lopsidedly and with great speed through the ancient pine floorboards.

Termites were responsible — white ants, if you like — but I have never lived down the stigma of being the guilty party who exposed the house for what it was, a mere shell of a suburban home honeycombed by a couple of billion very diligent white ants. Such guilt is a lifetime inheritance, which explains why I found it very hard to settle down and enjoy the scenery as Hugh trundled his four-wheel drive up the lonely spine of Cape York Peninsula into the fascinating world of the giant ant hill.

Well, they're ant hills to most of us, but entomologists, dinkum ant experts, call them termite mounds. No doubt most people making that fascinating trip up to the tip of the Cape for the first time are bowled over by the initial grandeur of the mounds — the size, the colour, the vast numbers. But after a couple of kilometres, well, you see one termite mound, you've seen them all.

But the thing that continued to capture me, despite the guilt complex, was the individually sculptured architecture of each one of the millions that cover the Cape. They looked like cathedrals in Cologne, castles in Spain, sharp spires and turrets, graceful single-columns and crowded colonnades. Down the dusty road a few kilometres they looked like shrouded medieval figures grouped in prayer, the light grey marble chiselled to perfection by the Old Masters.

A few more kilometres north the mounds changed shape again to look like the ant hills we know from less exotic parts of the state, monolithic blobs of dirt thrown up by none too artistic and certainly shoddy little termites, the lazy rotters.

I won't go into the details of what makes one breed of termite overwhelmingly more artistic than another because I don't know. But I can tell you, having talked to an entomologist, that there are about 250 breeds of termites up north, of which fewer than fifty live and build above the ground. The tallest mound recorded in Australia is a 6.5 metre skyscraper at Kakadu, but some of those we saw on the Cape would give that one a run for the money. Some are very old, maybe centuries old.

Many termite breeds are so smart they have the comfort of constant year-round temperatures. On mornings in summer they live and work in chambers within the thin outer western walls of their mounds while the sun beats down on the eastern walls. After midday they migrate to the shaded eastern wall. In winter, they reverse the process.

The fact that most termite breeds are grass-eaters and do not touch wood does little to protect householders if they use the wrong timber in their homes, because there are plenty of wood-eaters. Pioneers were quick to learn that termites would not eat certain timber, such as ironwood and cypress, after the unwary used any available timber and saw their fences and humpies eaten out almost as soon as they were constructed. The smart settlers who used unpalatable timber in their houses, sheds, yards and fences were unwittingly building monuments to their wisdom, for the basic solid frames of their structures still stand throughout the north more than a century on.

Pioneer Frank Jardine was such a man. The ironwood

yards he built at long-deserted Bertiehaugh Station would probably be intact today if it weren't for 104 years of bushfires and, more recently, the depredations of vandals who cut up the sturdy ironwood posts for fire-wood. Those that remain are as solid as the day Jardine and his men rammed them in.

Termites don't have to wait for a bloke to build timber structures before they can enjoy a feed on the house. There is a particularly hungry species that actually builds its mound around growing trees, encasing the trunk in a thin, airtight skin of moulded mud that inevitably becomes its death shroud. This brought the artist alive in Mr Sawrey because whole forests were liberally sprinkled with false trunks of vivid reds and yellows and dull greys and blacks, according to the colour of the soil. But nothing fascinated me like the cathedral- and statue-shaped termite mounds — authentic, mystical sculptures of nature. Travelling in such country, you don't have to wonder how the Dreamtime became so rich in spirit culture. There is a fortune to be made from those mounds for anyone who can move them, intact, a couple of thousand kilometres to the city. If I could do that I would send the garden gnome industry to the wall in a trice and make my fortune because any householder with a smidgin of culture would want one of nature's finest works for the front lawn.

So far the only person I know with termite mounds in his front yard is pioneering cattleman, Rod Heinemann, right up the Cape on Bramwell Station. When Rod took up Bramwell in the forties, he decided the giant red ant hills out the front of his homestead looked so good he left them there instead of knocking them down for a tennis court, as was the custom.

Today those giant red spires are an inspiring sight at dawn and dusk, standing guard over old Bramwell home-stead — so inspiring they have rid me of my forty-year-old white ant phobia to a point where I would need little encouragement to leap into a fiery fandango this very instant.

RIP DAY ON
THE WALLABY. CAPE YORK.

LAURA

On the Wallaby

We took the back tracks from one side of Cape York to the other hoping to bump into Roy Daly around one dusty bend or another. We didn't see him, but then Roy won't be meeting many people on the track he was tramping when Hugh and I were up that way recently. Roy was walking back to the Northern Territory from Laura, west of Cooktown, the same way he arrived there about fourteen years ago — on the wallaby with a swag, a rifle and some flour and salt in his tucker bag. No one seems to know why he left his job as caretaker of a property outside Laura, but they reckon he probably just had a gutful of civilisation after so many years so close to town and decided it was time to move on. He just mentioned he was walking back to the Territory one day and next thing he was gone.

No one up there is worried for his safety because Roy is a loner, an expert bushman and most of all a survivor. He's the sort of bloke who would have opened up that wild north country if he had been born 150 years ago. I imagine he would have been asked to join Leichhardt or Kennedy or the Jardine brothers on their expeditions into the Queensland of last century. You get a new respect for those old-time explorers when you travel the north and see what they faced in a day-to-day life in the wilderness with a horse and a rifle. No four-wheel drives, radio telephones, roadhouses, pubs or flying doctor for them.

Come to think of it that's how I imagine Roy will be

doing it overland today — pretty tough. Funny thing is locals around Laura don't want to talk much about Roy because he's the sort of bloke who might fly into a rage if he ever reads this. He just keeps himself to himself and if there's one thing northern people do extremely well it's respect the other joker's privacy. Besides, Roy's also the sort of bloke who might hold a grudge against anyone mentioning his name behind his back, or so they kept warning me. "Hey mate, don't use his name," or "Listen mate, don't quote me, hey?"

In a way I'm a bit of a bastard for even mentioning his name, although up that way it's not unusual for a man, or a woman for that matter, to change names from time to time. Anyway I'll be a couple of thousand miles away if Roy ever reads this and I reckon he'd be a real old man before he could walk to Brisbane and sort me out.

In fact there's really not much I can tell you about him except that he's a terrific bushman and worker if you leave him alone. He built a set of cattle yards on the property he managed that they reckon will stand straight and true long after the youngest among us is gone.

"They're bloody bewdy yards, mate, a real monument to what one man can do on his own," a bloke told us in Laura's tin pub, the Quinkin. "Posts and rails as thick as telegraph poles. You wonder how he did it on his own. But, hey, don't quote me, mate. Roy wouldn't like that."

Roy also worked on some yards in town one time. He used to start real early before the other workers arrived, but if he got there and found some other bloke had started before him he'd just go home. I don't know how far Roy will walk before he gets to wherever it is he's going, but you'll get some idea if you look at a map of Australia, put your finger on Laura just west of Cooktown and draw it across Queensland into the Territory, to Tennant Creek, say. Then you'll see it's a damn long way to walk, and swim too, because there are quite a few unbridged creeks and rivers to cross when you're overlanding it like Roy.

When we first heard about Roy's epic trek Hugh and I decided to drive across the bottom of Cape York Peninsula through Mt Surprise, Croydon, Normanton and Karumba, then take the back roads to Laura. It was quite a trip, and for the first couple of hundred kilometres I thought I saw Roy and his swag shimmering in the distant haze, but it always turned out to be a corner post or the rare signpost. Then we worked out a bloke like Roy certainly wouldn't be on the road, no sir. He'd be treading his own path somewhere, like all loners.

A couple of days later we saw a young bloke driving a bulldozer on a lonely road near Palmerville. It was a pretty unusual scene because he had his young son sitting on his lap pretending to drive the dozer. His wife was driving slowly behind in a 4WD. I guess they were heading back to camp for the weekend because it was a Friday afternoon. He'd heard of Roy Daly but reckoned we wouldn't see him if he saw us first, which was pretty likely. Anyway we got to Laura without sighting him.

One day we might catch up with Roy but I don't think I'll be able to find out much more about the man without him getting cranky and taking a swing at me, which no doubt will connect with devastating strength and accuracy. You don't want that, do you? I know I don't.

OUT OF FUEL ON WYAABA CREEK! CAPE YORK.

NORMANTON

Lure of the
Purple Pub

Is there anywhere else bar Australia where a man could
get stuck on the road for a couple of days on his way to
the local for a round or two with his mates? Such was the
plight in which Sawrey and I found Jimmy Whatsisname
camped on Wyaaba Creek about half way between his
home at Kowanyama Aboriginal community and his local,
the Purple Pub, 350 kilometres down the track at Normanton. Jimmy, his wife, his little piccaninny and his
mate had been waiting patiently beside their battered old
Ford by the creek bank after setting out two days earlier
to have a couple of cold beers at the Purple Pub.

They started the journey with a faith in providence that
this white man will never understand. For although there
are no petrol stations, hotels or corner stores on the lonely
road from Kowanyama to Normanton at the bottom of the
Gulf of Carpentaria, they had only enough petrol for half
the trip, no food and no shelter except for a couple of
towels slung over the boughs of a tree. Maybe some
Dreamtime spirit told them a generous and well-prepared
traveller like Hugh Sawrey would come along with some
spare petrol sooner or later, and it was just a matter of
time, of which they had plenty.

Then again, maybe Jimmy was only half joking when
he said with a smile he was about to see if the old bus
would run on creek water when we came along. I don't
understand such blind faith in providence, and I think I
never will. But it was no trouble at all to Jimmy, and even

when we pulled up to ask if he was in trouble, it was more at our instigation than his because he wasn't jumping up and down to grab our attention. He just gave us a half-wave and a huge grin and said he wouldn't mind a cold beer, but he'd settle for a bit of petrol if we had any to spare. So we gave them enough petrol for the trip, a loaf of bread, some canned food and milk and, for a minute there, Jimmy seemed pretty confident he was going to get a cold beer, too.

But fair go, Jimmy, old sport, getting a free fed and a half-tank of petrol in the middle of the wilderness isn't a bad effort in anyone's language. So we wished him well and said there was plenty of cold beer just down the road a couple of hundred kilometres at the Purple Pub, and his reply in a distinctly Aboriginal community accent was strange, but emphasised the influence of television in that timeless land: "Right on, man! Right on!" said Jimmy as he walked back into the shade, apparently in no hurry to get anywhere.

Not being in a hurry to get anywhere is part of life in the north. If you don't run out of petrol like Jimmy, then it rains and the rivers rise and cut you off for months on end. So you need to be patient, you learn to plait green-hide ropes in The Wet — or take up knitting. The bloke who talked about the north as a timeless land really knew what he was on about. Up there they don't ask you what time it is, rather what day it is. You can't walk into a pub or store without some bloke shouting out: "Hey mate, what's today?"

In all the timelessness and isolation there are some gentle reminders that modern travel has all but killed off that old cliché about the tyranny of distance, except in The Wet, of course. We pulled into Mount Surprise service station one thirsty Sunday arvo for a sandwich and a beer. The operator, Tracey Butler, said she didn't serve beer but if we'd hang on a sec, she'd rip into the pub next door and get us a couple of stubbies.

"It helps when you know the publican," she said. "He's me dad."

She seemed really pleased when Hugh told her she made the best tomato and onion sandwiches in Australia, bar none, and when she found out she was talking to Hugh Sawrey himself, she invited us to yarn with her parents Bruce and Neicy Butler, who were real fans. Neicy remembered Peacock, the old drover who was the subject of Sawrey's great work, "Peacock's Travelling Mob", which was raffled by the *Courier-Mail* to help Charleville flood victims in 1990.

A couple of days and about 700 kilometres later we were passing isolated Dunbar Station on the Gulf side of the Peninsula, and reckoned we might as well say hello to the grazier, Gordon Hamilton, and ask about the back road to Laura. Very few travellers had been that way since The Big Wet. Gordon was pretty busy trucking cattle so we excused ourselves after a couple of minutes, and just as we were leaving a female voice yelled down from the road train: "Gidday, Mr Sawrey." We looked up and there was a pretty girl covered in red dust smiling among the wild-eyed cattle.

Who the hell's that? Hugh whispered to me out the corner of his mouth. Search me, said I.

"Remember me?" she said. "I'm the best tomato and onion sandwich maker in Australia, bar none."

Sure enough, it was Tracey from far-off Mount Surprise. She'd flown a tiny 150 Cessna into Dunbar that day to see her boyfriend, Peter Vickers, a road-train operator from Cloncurry.

"I wouldn't see much of Peter if I couldn't fly because it's about 900 kilometres by road from Mount Surprise to Cloncurry," said Tracey. And Brisbane blokes think they're long-distance lovers when they live at Chermside and their girlfriends live at Mount Gravatt. Whenever she gets a chance, and there isn't too much spare time when you own and operate a service station outback, Tracey finds out where Peter is headed with his road train and flies there to meet him.

"We see each other once or twice a month, thanks to that little plane. It would be very difficult without it."

Meanwhile I can't tell you what happened to Jimmy Whatsisname on the track down the Gulf to the Purple Pub. But when he gets there I can guarantee the beer will be cold. They don't give it a chance to get warm out there.

"Camp-oven and Billy-can"

BRAMWELL
PACK HORSES
CAPE YORK

LAWREY
'91

Dirt Floors and Death Adders

Don't kid yourself in this space age that the last of the Aussie pioneers died out with moleskin trousers and cabbage-tree hats. There were fair dinkum pioneers in Queensland right through to the seventies doing it just as tough as our great-grandfathers did it a century before.

One of our pioneers is old Rod Heinemann of Bramwell station, who is still fencing and mustering and doing most of the things he did to tame his patch of the Peninsula back in the forties and fifties. The remarkable thing about Rod is that he has survived the crocs, the taipans, the death adders and the almost total early isolation for 83 years. The other remarkable thing about meeting Rod Heinemann is getting him to talk about a life spent entirely north of Coen, his birthplace.

You see, Rod's a shy bloke who likes to be sure he's talking to genuine people, and I believe that doesn't include journalists. He met one years ago and wasn't impressed.

"That bloke mucked up everything I said. I haven't trusted them since," Rod said.

At times like these it helps to have a joker like Hugh at your side who knows the bush inside out and talks the language. And a bottle of rum never goes astray either.

After a couple of hefty nips, and with Hugh spinning yarns about cattle camps from the Channel Country to the Gulf, Rod recalled an early life that was every bit as rugged, isolated and primitive as that of the pioneers. He was born to horses, was a stockman from his early teens, and always worked the Peninsula. In his eighty-three years he's been to Cairns a couple of times and once made it to Townsville but that's as far south as he wanted to go and he reckons he's not likely to venture "south" again.

Old Rod took up Bramwell, a 1350 square kilometre station, in 1941 when it was just a shack with a dirt floor in the middle of the scrub; no power, no refrigeration, no telephone — no link whatsoever with the outside world. If you got crook you just had to look after yourself until you got better . . . if you got better. That's the way he got over a redback spider bite way back. "I was pretty crook for a while, but I came good in the end."

He recalled a night around a droving campfire years ago when a death adder crawled silently over a stock-man's swag. Death adders aren't supposed to wander around at night. "Everyone in the camp hung their mos-quito nets up that night and tucked them very, very tight under their swags," Rod said.

Every Boxing Day right up to the seventies, Rod and a team of ten to fifteen Aboriginal stockmen would drive big mobs of cattle 650 kilometres down the road to market at Mareeba; well, not exactly down the road because there were no roads as such. He'd drive the mob down the overland telegraph line which linked the tip of the Cape with Brisbane, picking up neighbours' cattle on the way on a contract-droving basis. Why a Boxing Day start? He wanted to have Christmas at home with his family.

The trip down was painfully slow and averaged nine weeks. But with the mob safely delivered at Mareeba they'd make it home to Bramwell in just three weeks, three months on the road in all. Rod Heinemann made that odyssey twice a year for more than thirty years while his wife, Theresa, looked after the family and kept the property running.

How did they do the shopping in such circumstances? Well, twice a year, a supply ship sailed down the Gulf of Carpentaria from Thursday Island and delivered the goods at a small wharf forty-five kilometres up the Ducie

River. Three days before it was due to arrive, Rod mustered a team of forty-two packhorses and pushed them through sixty kilometres of the rough, broken country that separated Bramwell from the small bush landing. A week later he would arrive back at Bramwell homestead with his packhorse team carrying the produce of a six-month shopping list. If you forgot the salt you did without it for the next six months.

I neglected to ask Rod if he ever forgot the rum. But then that would have been such a monumental catastrophe I guess he would have mentioned it without prompting.

Theresa still makes out a six-month shopping list but it comes in by road from Cairns these days. Things are gradually changing on Bramwell Station — as they are right up the Peninsula — with the cattle industry struggling and tourism becoming a viable alternative. Under Theresa's astute eye, Bramwell is an overnight stop for the many four-wheel-drive tour operators who make the run from Cairns and Cooktown to the Tip in the dry season. She has battled to put in comfortable prefabricated cabins and supervises genuine home-cooked bush tucker for visitors up to five nights a week at the peak of the season.

It's tough going in this economic climate, but then Rod and Theresa are battlers who've had it tough all their lives. Despite his age, Rod just keeps going like a mechanical man. Like I was saying earlier, Rod, Hugh and I knocked over a bottle of rum the night we arrived at Bramwell. Next day, as I blinked painfully at my portable computer and it blinked mockingly back at me, old Rod walked off into the scrub, barefoot among the snakes and centipedes as always, to put up another couple of chains of barbed wire fencing before dark.

If anyone ever tells you Aussie pioneers died out with cabbage-tree hats and moleskin trousers, tell 'em to put their money where their mouth is and call me in a hurry — because I like a quick quid as much as the next joker.

"CORN BEEF AND DAMPER — THAT'S THE GO!"

CAPE YORK PENINSULA

Corned Beef Blues

You've seen the size of the bullocks going round the Brisbane Ekka in the grand parade umpteen times, haven't you? Righto! Take the biggest beast there, put it to sleep permanently with a thump behind the ears and dress and quarter him. Now picture one of those hind quarters on a butcher's hook, and that's roughly the size of the piece of corned beef Sawrey had slung over his shoulder when he came staggering out of the butcher shop in Karumba. Hugh likes his corned beef.

"Corned beef and damper, that's the go, mate," he often says, and I agree. But when you've dined on corned beef exclusively for a couple of weeks, even when it's been cleverly blended with cornflakes, tinned prunes or anything else that comes to hand in the dark, it really is too much of a good thing. Worse, it can be an extreme health hazard, forcing one to risk life and limb trying to catch a fish or two for a change of diet.

It was to this end that we were camped under a tropical canopy by a clear but sinister-looking creek about half way between Cairns and the Gulf. We had unrolled our swags on the bank, eaten a hearty lunch of corned beef and were now bobbing lines in the dark water. Crocodiles didn't worry us because this was fresh water and many kilometres from the coast. Fish didn't bother us either, in fact not at all, but this could hardly dampen the enthusiasm we experienced soon after wetting our lines when Hugh suddenly yelled: "Crikey, mate! Take a look at this!"

There at the end of his line, just below the surface, was the biggest freshwater prawn I've ever seen, at least a foot long. My reflex action was to smash the butt of my old rod down exactly where the prawn had been a split second before, but at least a hundred miles from where it was now. Having established that freshwater prawns are miles faster than our reflexes, we looked for smarter methods than brute force. This is a clever country, after all, and we soon discovered the prawns were real mugs because no matter how close I got with my waddy, the stupid things came straight back for more of the dead mullet on offer. They were crazy for it.

Dillies would be the answer, we reckoned, but with no strong wire to construct a hoop for a sugarbag dilly, we were temporarily frustrated until . . . until, with typical bushcraft that got us out of many a tight corner on the trip, we found a substitute; and not a length of the cocky's No. 8 fencing wire, as you might think. No, sir! Getting to our creekbank campsite, we'd had to cut and bulldoze our way through heavy vine, so we cut down lengths of it now and fashioned hoops for our dillies, baited them and dropped them over the bank. It was just a matter of boiling the billy and biding our time now, so Hugh filled in the interval with a great impersonation of the Bush Tucker Man, chewing pieces of bark, tasting berries, picking up ants and insects and telling an imaginary camera-microphone what real good tucker it was.

After a decent time, and when our billy was bubbling just so, we carefully pulled up our dillies. Nothing. We repeated this process for a couple of hours, then went back to serious line-fishing because I didn't like the sound of Hugh steeling his knife to carve out yet another corned beef dinner.

Then, just on sundown, action at last. We hauled two fish in at once. Two estuarine catfish, to be exact. This caused Hugh and me to look at each other in a curious way because we knew we had but a single thought: if estuarine catfish were in this sinister creek — becoming much more sinister now that the sun was setting — then it would also be home sweet home to estuarine crocodiles, the worst kind of crocodile. I don't know what the speed record is for breaking camp at sundown, but we would have given it a fair shake. Sure, it was a nice camp, but wo just knew there was a better one down the road somewhere that wasn't within a bull's roar of water

A few nights later, over a beer with grazier David Arnold of Wrotham Park Station, he reckoned we had done the right thing shifting camp. "You shouldn't trust any rivers or creeks in the far north," he said. "And you don't catch freshwater prawns in dillies made from that rotten, lousy, (expletive) rubber vine either. They shy clear of that stinking vine and its sap."

Peninsula cattlemen wish they could shy clear of rubber vine too, but it's up there to stay, thousands upon thousands of hectares of it, and spreading like cancer. In recent years it has become a major threat to the northern cattle industry — thick enough to choke off whole water courses. It's costing graziers in other ways too. Today the cost of mustering cattle by helicopter has become so high they would like to return to traditional ways.

Well, I asked, horseback was good enough for your fathers, so why not you?

"Because you can't ride a bloody horse through the bloody vine, that's why," said David.

It's a major problem in a myriad of headaches facing far-northern cattlemen. Like most environmental hazards it was imported — brought in by a Charters Towers resident who thought it would make a pretty garden hedge, it was. What a great pity the person wasn't clever enough to give it a big miss, like the freshwater prawn.

"SOMERSET
MEMORIAL"
CAPE YORK

SAWREY
'91

SOMERSET

Frank Jardine's Forgotten Frontier

Imagine an upside-down Queensland with most of the population crammed into Cape York Peninsula, and Brisbane a quaint country town in the south. Just think what might have been if history had followed the visions of governors, premiers, explorers, business men and speculators who from the earliest days of white settlement saw Cape York as the gateway to Australia. It was another Singapore, a South Seas crossroads of world commerce at the very tip of a brand new state. The vision was up and running in March 1863 when the newly appointed Government Resident, John Jardine, led a party of Royal Marines ashore on a headland at Somerset, overlooking Torres Strait, just east of the tip of Cape York.

A town plan was laid out and seventy blocks snapped up by speculators 2700 kilometres away in Brisbane, hoping to cash in on the new pearl of the Pacific. Thus were laid the foundations of what should have become the capital of Queensland, if not Australia, and possibly one of the South Pacific's richest trading posts. Alas, success is measured not in faded history or past adventures, but in mortar and brick, power and glory. Somerset was destined to become rich in the former and a broken-down pauper in the latter. It bloomed for a few years of lavish official entertainment for grand visitors, but faded to become the isolated paradise of one of Queensland's forgotten adventurers, Frank Jardine.

Today it is a crying shame that this priceless piece of

Queensland history has all but disappeared, not reclaimed by the jungle but destroyed by years of government neglect and yobbo vandalism. A tall white cross, three cannon, a plaque and a gateway arch are all that remain of a once-thriving outpost. Below on the foreshore the graves of Frank Jardine and his royal Samoan wife, Sana Solia, have survived years of vandalism and neglect, but only just.

Had Somerset become another Singapore, Frank Jardine would have been as much acclaimed in Queensland today as Sir Stamford Raffles, who is remembered in Singapore by statue, monument and the famed hotel. Instead Jardine, a larger-than-life Queensland explorer, adventurer and pioneer, lies in an unkempt grave in an almost inaccessible and deserted outpost.

I would never have reached Somerset, and certainly not the beachside graves, had it not been for Hugh Sawrey. Just one creek crossing between Bamaga and Somerset would have prevented me because a bridge had collapsed, leaving a sheer 1.5 metre drop at each end. I wanted to turn back but Hugh, an experienced four-wheel-drive operator, wouldn't listen. The risk was worth it, even the nightmare drive down a washed-out track from the residency ruins to the graves.

It is hard separating fact from fiction about Frank Jardine because much conjecture has been written. But his ten-month expedition with his young brother Alick from Rockhampton to Somerset in 1864–65 is authentic. Considering their ages, twenty-two and twenty years respectively, and their uncharted route through hostile Aboriginal territories up the Queensland coast, it was an epic and significant trek.

The Cape became a lifelong home to Frank Jardine. There he established the pearling industry, pioneered the cattle industry, explored Torres Strait, found pirate treasure, entertained the passing VIP parade lavishly and appears to have set himself up as the great white hunter and father protector of the north, bringing summary justice to all he surveyed, white man as well as black.

Jardine is credited with bringing blackbirders, pirates and escaped convicts, as well as headhunters and warring Aborigines, to his form of justice. He is reported to have found half a tonne of pirate treasure on a coral atoll, part of which he had made into a silver service used by VIP visitors at lavish, sometimes vice-regal dinners.

He was a fanatic on stone structures and built many grand stairways and sweeping paths and gardens around Somerset. At one stage he established a cattle property at Bertiehaugh, approximately two hundred kilometres south of Somerset, and it is a very strange experience to stumble on the remains of that isolated site in thick scrub and find extensive stone paths, gardens and a huge, stone-wall well among the ruins. The well is of particular interest, featuring hip-high surrounding walls which could have protected a couple of dozen riflemen in a last-ditch stand against attacking Aborigines.

Jardine abandoned Bertiehaugh after a few years to return to Somerset. Today locals believe constant Aboriginal raids on the homestead and crocodile attacks on his cattle forced him to leave. Hugh and I fished the Ducie River directly in front of the Bertiehaugh ruins, and if you can imagine a more likely spot for crocodile attacks, I'd like to hear about it.

The Jardine adventures would not seem complete without a great sea drama. So it came as no surprise to hear that Jardine was one of the first people involved in rescuing survivors from the passenger ship *Quetta*, which sank in 1890 just a few kilometres from Somerset. Jardine also broke the sad news to the rest of the world.

Few Queenslanders I've heard about could match Jardine for colour and dash in the most adventurous period in this state's history. With a little luck today he could have been peering across Torres Strait from a grand marble pedestal set in the heart of the rich and thriving metropolis of Somerset, capital and financial heart of Queensland. Instead he lies in a vandalised grave in the ruins of a mighty vision in one of the most inaccessible outposts of the state. What a crying shame.

BAMAGA, SEISIA

Northern Nightmares

The last kilometre of the seemingly endless journey from civilisation to the tip of Cape York must be made on foot and never, never make it without a trusty oyster knife. The rocky foreshores of that rugged finger of Queensland which finally drops away to combine the Coral and Arafura seas as Torres Strait, are lined with the biggest, sweetest oysters known. They come in shells like saucers and you munch them down at an average of three juicy bites to the oyster.

After three dozen of these, or maybe five, mixed in with the usual shell fragments and sand which accompany oysters eaten off the rocks, I wasn't feeling crash hot. But I was in better shape than the once-perfect hunting knife Hugh foolishly lent me to chisel through to such culinary delights.

That night in my swag under a lady apple tree on the beach at Seisia, outside Bamaga, I had nightmares about killer crocodiles and grotesque women, and awoke at one stage with what appeared to be a heart attack. I put this down to evil spirits haunting our camp because the sitting platform on which we had laid out our swags — to be out of reach of crocodiles — was a meeting place where Torres Strait Islanders had gathered for years to talk about a past rich in good and evil spirits. It was a frightening experience, lying awake under a pitch-black night with ancient spirits hurling searing aches and pains through my wretched body.

At dawn I groaned out my poor state of health to Sawrey, mentioning the nightmares and the evil spirits that had come down through the centuries to haunt me in this hallowed place. More like too many evil oysters, was his only reply. And once again he was correct. Three dozen giant oysters, maybe five, plus sand and grit, are more than enough to do terrible damage without the help of ancient spirits. Not that the far north is without a rich heritage in the spirit world, both in Torres Strait and Aboriginal cultures. Fortunately for outsiders, the good and bad spirits are easily identifiable. "The little round tubby fellas are the bad buggers, bouncing round everywhere," an ancient Aboriginal elder told me later. "The long skinny fellas are real good blokes." He'd had his share of experiences with the little round fellas, this old man, but more thanks to the white man's spirits than any from his Dreamtime, he said.

Many years ago he used to believe in the white man's ways, particularly when, as a sixteen-year-old stockman, he was summoned to town by the local police sergeant to marry the girl of his dreams. In those days whole Aboriginal tribes sometimes were moved from one district to another on the instructions of southern bureaucrats. So the young bloke was very happy to be riding into town for the wedding — until he got to the police station for the ceremony, that is. There he found he was set to marry the young sister of the girl of his dreams.

Why the mix-up? According to this old man sitting under a northern mango tree telling me about Aboriginal life fifty years ago, his brand-new fiancée was making terrible trouble for everyone in town, including the police, and they wanted to get rid of her. So, on the sergeant's insistence, my ancient friend married her. She signed her name inside a horseshoe the sergeant had drawn on a piece of paper, and he made a thumbprint on the same.

And what about his one true love, the elder sister? Said the old man with a faraway look in his fading eyes: "We saw each other after the wedding and she said she was sorry what happened. So was I. But we said we would still be good friends." So the town lost its headache, but I gather it was a long, long time before my ancient friend lost his.

I didn't hear any similar stories up on the Tip around Bamaga, but the centre itself was established with a little help from bureaucrats soon after the Second World War. Bamaga and nearby Seisia are the only two Torres Strait Islander communities on the Queensland mainland, and were set up by the state government, with permission from local Aborigines, when one of the most northern Torres Strait islands, Saibai, was inundated by a flood tide in 1946. The majority of Saibai islanders were brought to the mainland on government boats, but a group of six families, under a fiercely independent leader named Mugai Elu, sailed down in their own lugger and settled on a beautiful beach at Red Island Point. They called it Seisia, derived from the first letter of the surnames of the six original families.

Today, under Elu's son Joseph, Seisia is a most progressive mainland community and one of only two with camping facilities for southern tourists. Joseph Elu recognises the future of tourism in the far north and is gearing up to cater for the undoubted explosion in the future. His camping ground on the ocean is at the hub of the two major tourist attractions at the Tip — Thursday Island, seventy-five minutes away by water taxi, and Somerset about an hour away by road. The camping ground is managed by former hunting and fishing guide Gary Wright, a naturalist and local historian who has been living in the far north since the sixties.

Does he ever plan to leave Seisia? Not really, he says. "In fact, I've picked out the very sandhill where I want to be buried."

"QUETTA
MEMORIAL CHURCH
THURSDAY ISLAND.

THURSDAY ISLAND

Cissy "Quetta" Brown

If you equate the demon booze with the forces of darkness then the devil and the Lord are level-pegging in the battle for the living souls of Queensland's last frontier, Thursday Island. Each has assembled a four-pronged force on that compelling, faraway island in the form of four pubs lining up against four churches. Who is in front on TI's scoreboard of life? An intensive personal inspection revealed the pubs are very popular indeed. But the ecclesiastical team has a real winner in the Anglican church which is not only officially the nation's smallest cathedral, but also its most interesting.

The tiny Quetta All Souls Memorial Cathedral, consecrated in 1893, is a living memorial to one of Australia's worst maritime disasters in which the British India Company's barquentine-rigged steamer, RMS *Quetta*, went down in Torres Strait with 134 souls on the peaceful, moonlit night of 28 February 1890. It is hard to imagine the sudden disaster on the bright, calm night described by the majority of the 158 survivors all those years ago.

It was just after nine p.m. Women were in the music room singing round a piano. Passengers were writing letters home, to be posted next day at Thursday Island, the *Quetta*'s last Aussie port of call on its way from Brisbane to London. Many other passengers had gone below for the night when a "slight grating noise" was heard. For some passengers strolling on the deck it sounded like an anchor dropping into a calm sea. There was little concern and those who expressed surprise were quickly reassured by more experienced travellers and crew.

But down below the full horror of the slight impact was being witnessed by the engine room crew as an uncharted pinnacle of rock pierced the iron hull, carving a hole fifty-three metres long and two metres wide beneath their feet. The ship had been travelling at about eleven knots and the rock sliced through the iron sheeting like a can-opener through a sardine tin. It took just three minutes for the *Quetta* to disappear forever, just a few kilometres off the tip of Cape York.

There are many poignant stories about the tragedy in a book called *The Quetta* by Captain John Foley, a Torres Strait pilot, but none more so than the fate of the only child to survive the disaster. She went to her grave fifty-nine years later in Southport with a borrowed name and no inkling of her true identity.

Other survivors could not identify the child, but it was thought she may have been the granddaughter of a man in Scotland; so money was raised at Thursday Island by public subscription to send her there. For reasons unknown she never made the trip and was adopted by Thursday Island pilot, Capt. Edmund Brown and his wife, Marjorie. Curiously, they christened her Cecil Lechmere Brown, but she became known as Cissy within the family. However, almost from the time she arrived at Thursday Island after the sinking she was nicknamed "Quetta" by the public, a name taken up by the press and one that stuck, although her adopted family tried their best to block out all memory of the disaster.

She left Thursday Island at the turn of the century after the death of her foster father and was brought to Brisbane by the family of his brother, Villiers Brown, a successful business man. She married twice, her first husband having been killed in an accident at Clayfield in 1917. She lived at various times at Knobble Creek, near Dayboro, Bald Hills and Southport. Although Cissy "Quetta" Brown died not knowing who she was, the search for her identity continues today. Old photos of her and a child passenger named Mary Copeland are being scientifically studied in an attempt to solve the mystery 100 years later.

No doubt Cissy "Quetta" Brown returned to Thursday Island during her lifetime, maybe searching for her identity in the peace and memories of tiny Quetta Cathedral. If she did she would have had plenty to remind her of the disaster. As well as being a quaint little church, it is a museum of *Quetta* memorabilia, starting with the ship's bell hanging from a scaffold outside the church. Inside are a coral-encrusted porthole salvaged from the ship, a stern riding lamp, and a lifebuoy; a saloon table top forms part of the high altar.

The cathedral also contains many memorials including stained glass windows donated by some of Queensland's leading families whose relatives were among the victims, for the *Quetta* was a fashionable liner with the well-to-do. Not surprisingly the nautical theme prevails inside the little cathedral with photos of the *Quetta*; the stained glass depicts its sinking as well as several sailing ships, turtles and an octopus. A most unusual cathedral is Quetta All Souls Memorial and, like Thursday Island itself, it is an experience not to be missed by anyone with a feeling for Queensland history.

Thursday Island is a township and community with the look and feel of a typical Queensland coastal village of the thirties and forties; certainly a lot like I remember Yeppoon to be, growing up there during the war — rusty iron buildings, a little dusty, a little tumble-down, where nothing seems to get out of second gear except when locals occasionally fire up on the evils of John Barleycorn or fall prey to the temptations of Eve. But God is in there today with an even chance, like I said. Four churches lining up against four pubs will do me for a fair fight.

THURSDAY ISLAND

Somerset Maugham Lives

Thursday Island and Torres Strait have a deadly, romantic attraction that must be seen and felt because it defies description. Writers have been drawn to and captured by that most beautiful slice of Queensland since the coming of the whites, but I have yet to read an accurate description of the "feel" of the place. As a matter of fact I reckoned for a moment there recently, standing on the wide veranda of TI's Grand Hotel looking across Torres Strait, that I might invoke the spirit of the great W. Somerset Maugham for the answer.

You see, Maugham used to live and write in the room next to mine in the old Grand, a sound wooden wall between us, which is as it should be from what I've heard of the old fruit. He wrote two highly successful short stories in that room and no doubt spent many hours gazing out across the incredibly blue water waiting for inspiration, as I did recently. He would have sipped drinks there for sure, although from something more elegant than my brown stubbie. It wasn't hard to imagine that the spirit of the long-dead author was alive and kicking on that cool veranda because his corner room had been turned into a memorial to him and is permanently held ready and waiting in case he returns from wherever it is dead writers go.

It's a good feeling to know you are in the presence of a literary giant, even if it is only in spirit, and the feeling gets stronger as the line of empty stubbies expands down such a weathered veranda. Old pubs set the pace for invoking the past — the creaking floors, the rattling walls. What stories a century-old pub like the Grand could tell of the pearling days when TI was the centre of the romantic South Seas!

I was thinking these thoughts as I went to bed that night and blow me down if the spirit of W. Somerset Maugham didn't come clattering through the wall just about midnight. Well, it sounded like the spirit of W. Somerset Maugham but when I awoke it was only another guest pounding the wall with what sounded like the back of an axe trying to stop me snoring — I've rather an astonishing snore in the dead of night if you're not expecting it.

Next day I was paying a heavy price for attempting to invoke the author's spirit and was standing shakily outside a rusty store trying to quell the fire with lemonade, when a most disturbing interview came over a nearby ghetto-blaster. It was all about the damage alcohol does to the liver and brain. No better place for such a show than thirsty far north Queensland, say I. The radio expert had dealt with irreparable liver damage and was laying it on thick about memory loss when the broadcast became a reality for me. For as I stared into space trying not to listen, a shiny hire car pulled up, a polished Islander in a fashionable tropical suit bounced out beaming and shook me by the hand.

"Lawrie, old mate! What do you know! How are you? How about a drink?" he said at once, like we were long lost friends.

I looked at him closely and instantly knew it was true what they said about memory loss for I was observing a man I could swear I had never seen before. After assuring him I was well and enjoying myself on TI, the neat black stranger bounced back into the car and drove off.

That night I stood on the very spot on the veranda where I imagined Somerset Maugham would have stood half a century earlier worrying desperately about whether he too suffered acute memory loss. I had left off invoking

the spirits of dead writers and was concentrating my
hardest on who in the hell the neatly dressed stranger
was, and seriously considering committing myself to a
dog pound for safe keeping.

Here, obviously, was the sad case of a whole chapter
missing from a man's life. From here on it would be one
long series of total strangers lining up to say hello to the
man without a memory. But next day all was revealed
when a local official identified the stranger as the council
chairman I had interviewed on remote Boigu Island earlier in the week. For while he was dressed to kill on TI, he
was unrecognisable as the bloke dressed island fashion,
in ragged football jersey, tattered shorts, barefoot, and on
a rusty bike back on Boigu.

Memory-loss traumas with such happy endings de-
serve to be celebrated, so that sundown I was back on the
veranda staring out to sea in between nibbling nervous
noggins and attempting to conjure up dead writers' spirits. It's beautiful looking across the Strait outside Somerset Maugham's room at the Grand. To your right the
sun is just down behind the dark green islands. The rest
is just one tranquil sweep of clear blue water dotted here
and there with boats, even a couple of graceful old
pearling luggers.

There's something else about it too, something sinister
— a lurking danger perhaps. And just when there seemed
nothing on earth that could disturb this incredible scene
of peace and beauty, I think old Somerset sent me a sign.
For there, in the mirror-like surface of the darkening
waters less than 200 metres away, suddenly appeared
the chilling dorsal fin and tail of a large shark. It moved
slowly, lazily, just under the still surface for so long my
initial sense of danger was replaced by an admiration for
the sleek and graceful creature.

Suddenly, as if deliberately shattering this soft twilight
in paradise, the shark thrashed itself into a frenzy of
killing as it flailed its way repeatedly through a school of
small fish just a few metres offshore.

It was all over in a couple of minutes and paradise

returned to peace and tranquillity once more. To me that was the "feel" of Thursday Island and Torres Strait. It's a beautiful, compelling, romantic, deadly place that you have to feel for yourself, because no one can truly describe it. Not even W. Somerset Maugham and certainly not me.

"GRAVE OF A PIONEER"
CAPE YORK

BOIGU ISLAND

The Tree of Skull

You tread warily broaching the subject of heritage when the gentleman you are talking to quietly under the coconut tree numbers head hunters among his ancestors. But the council chairman of this most northerly slice of Queensland, and Australia for that matter, does not mind in the least, thank heavens.

"Why should we? It's part of our history," said Donald Banu, chairman of Boigu Island, about 150 kilometres north of Thursday Island and just a couple away from Papua New Guinea. "We want to pass our history on to our children, along with old skills like carving and weaving."

Naturally the time for taking heads has long gone but it is hard to visit this remote island and not be reminded it was once home to the most feared warriors of Torres Strait. One of the most honoured places in the 300-strong village is a wild almond tree which once bore very strange fruit. It is aptly named and clearly marked "Tree of Skull" and it was from this tree the Boigu warriors hung heads sliced mostly from the shoulders of their Papua New Guinea neighbours just seven kilometres to the north. There was great ceremony to the taking of heads, from the preparation of the raid to the final scraping, smoking, and curing on the "Tree of Skull".

Why make such a fuss over someone's head, you ask? For starters, successful head hunting brought great honour to a young warrior, not to mention wealth. Heads were valuable currency, particularly for trading back to other PNG tribes for such commodities as the giant logs used in making the dugout canoes that still ply Torres Strait.

Why didn't the Boigu warriors chop down their own trees and let their PNG neighbours keep their heads, you ask? It's a question you wouldn't need to ask if you were to visit Boigu Island. Boigu is a long, flat slab of mud on clay, barely rising above sea level and covered mainly with mangroves. In a nutshell it's mudcrab and mozzie country. What little sand filters to shore through the mud is mostly grabbed by locals to spread around their walkways because they're muddy murder in the wet season. That's the downside of the Boigu Island story, but Queensland's most northerly citizens seem pretty happy with their lot.

This is "mañanaland", tomorrow country, so you have to be wary of statistics around here. The people of the far north and Torres Strait in particular — black, white and brindle — don't measure time in minutes, days or centuries, and the same goes for distances and numbers of just about any sort. As one bloke said: "We know about one, two or maybe three people, but after that it doesn't matter much. It just becomes a whole lot of people." The most northerly Queenslanders of Boigu Island had been on their island home for many centuries collecting heads before Anglican missionaries sailed through the Strait converting the islanders to Christianity in 1871. That anniversary is celebrated as the "Coming of the Light" on 1 July each year. And they must have done an excellent job of marketing Jesus Christ because today Boigu islanders not only do not cut off their neighbours' heads but would have to be among Queensland's most devout Christians. Not all the islanders are daily churchgoers but the corrugated iron church is mostly packed for morning and evening prayers and overflowing for Sunday services.

One still and misty morning I looked in on the early daily service, this enduring evidence of the coming of the white world to Torres Strait, but there was no getting away from the past. They sang their hymns not to the strains of an organ, although they have one, or guitars, of which there are many, but to the haunting, eerie beat of an ancient island drum, the like of which I had never heard. It was compelling stuff, listening to that timeless drum while standing under the "Tree of Skull" not thirty metres from the altar of Christianity.

I came to Boigu Island with the good intention of not mentioning head hunting in case it offended the locals. Thank heavens it doesn't, as it would be impossible to visit and not be reminded of the past. Even on distant Thursday Island there is a barman from this area with hair knotted in a tight bun on top of his head who, when angry with his customers, will yell in frustration: "Fifty years ago I would have eaten you."

What will happen on Boigu Island is anyone's guess, for television arrived back in 1991 and already you are more likely to hear one of the handsome Boigu kids singing "Oh! What a feeling" in the schoolyard than beating a drum or carving traditional figures from pig tusks, wood, dugong bone or pearl shell. Such skills are disappearing with the ageing of frail old men like Abia Ingui, an eighty-four-year-old master craftsman I met sitting cross-legged on a bench carving a dugong bone.

People like chairman Banu are keen to get youngsters interested in old crafts and old men like Ingui are keen to teach. But how do you get the kids interested in old crafts and values now that television has arrived? Any scheme will need to be more successful than Banu's attempt to clean up the island and earn the council some money by collecting aluminium cans. Banu placed drums around the village and asked the people to drop their cans in for resale on the mainland. About the same time a brand new craze swept Boigu with people cutting aluminium cans into shiny flowers and stars and nailing them to coconut trees. The used-can business didn't get off the ground.

The uncertain future for these most northerly Queenslanders is that their remote island has scant prospect of providing little more than menial work for the scores of kids who start out with no English in the island's modern primary school and graduate to high schools on Thursday

Island and the mainland. It matters little how well they cope at high school, because there seems little chance they can return to their birthplace with hopes of fulfilling employment ambitions.

The Boigu situation is not unique. It is repeated throughout the Strait islands. They're right, you know. The far north gets to you after a while. But these days you at least walk away with your head where it should be.

SAIBAI ISLAND

Stranded on Saibai

Having studied the situation first hand, it is my considered opinion that tourism will give the remote northern islands of Torres Strait a big miss for a few years yet — and the locals should be grateful for such an optimistic forecast. This opinion swamped me as I stood alone and soaked under a coconut tree on a remote mangrove island, mudstained up to the knees, luggage awash, clutching an airline ticket for a plane that didn't arrive — and with the next flight five days away.

It was not a pretty sight, this distressed traveller slouched beside the unsealed airstrip on Saibai Island, a little slice of Queensland mud just south of Papua New Guinea. Realistically, I should not complain because travel in remote areas always depends on the weather. Just the same, when you've got a valid airline ticket in your hand and a tight schedule to meet back in civilisation, it is easy to forget yourself. But not before my soaked spirits soared as I heard my plane's engines grow louder through the clouds. I've always said there's nothing like the sound of your plane approaching when all you want to do is get going . . . nothing, that is, except the sound of your plane growing fainter in the distance, leaving you stranded on a muddy island like Saibai.

Luckily there was a public phone box on the island and it was there I learned from an airline official on Thursday

Island that the pilot of my lost flight had considered it too dangerous to land on the mud strip. But not to worry, he said, there's a plane out tomorrow. Oh dear, it's booked solid, but we can get you out in five days.

Five days on a remote island like Saibai can be tough because they don't cater for unexpected travellers. Anyone who goes to an island community needs permissiom from the local council first and can then arrange accommodation. The limited accommodation is usually booked by visiting government officials, public servants and tradesmen. By the way, it was one of my big disappointments in Torres Strait to find that rather than train home-grown skilled workers, tradesmen regularly fly in from TI to do what would normally be considered handyman chores on government installations. Worse, tradesmen's trips are often costly disasters when they arrive with the wrong replacement parts caused by confused signals.

Back in the phone box on Saibai Island, the airline official at the other end was saying there was an alternative to sleeping under a coconut tree for five days. I could charter a plane and be back in civilisation in a jiffy, he said, weather permitting of course. Just give us a call in a couple of hours with a local weather report.

I learned a lot about reading weather and airstrip conditions over the next couple of hours and was brimming with reports from a dozen locals who confirmed my opinion that the airstrip was safe. My man on TI wasn't easily convinced, though. He asked how high the clouds were. How should I know? I said. I'm not an expert on clouds. Well, stick your head out the phone box and have a guess. They look pretty high to me, I said. He asked if I could see New Guinea. Can we see New Guinea? I asked an islander walking past the phone box. That's it over there, he said, pointing through some coconut trees.

Thanks mate, I said, and please don't go away for a while, hey? I told the man I could see New Guinea. Well, is it clearing in the southeast? Is it clearing in the southeast? I asked the man outside. It was, and the wind was from the south, there was a break in the clouds to the east, the sea had settled down in the west and the airstrip was definitely firm to holding, all of which information came from the man waiting patiently outside.

Later that afternoon my plane made a beautiful sight coming out of the clouds, which were more high than low in my estimation. We won't talk about the cost; it is the sort of thing that is always on the cards in that part of Queensland, and a good thing too if it means keeping tourists at bay.

Of course tourists are rarely seen outside Thursday Island, so it's not an issue with most islanders, although the council chairman on beautiful Dauan Island, Phillip Biggie, is aware of his island's potential as a small but exclusive tourist destination. Dauan, Saibai and Boigu islands form the most northern Torres Strait communities, hanging just off PNG, but there the similarity ends. Dauan, a remnant of the Great Divide, is like a palm-fringed paradise of hills and valleys after the muddy flatness of Boigu and Saibai. The difference also seems to be reflected in the neatness of the village and the attitude of the people on Dauan. Chairman Biggie runs a pretty tight ship — there is no wet canteen and villagers observe a voluntary community work-for-the-dole system that seems to work.

One other thing the three communities do have in common, and it probably applies throughout Torres Strait, is the islanders' liking for processed tinned sea-foods, like smoked oysters, crab meat and fish. How can they have such poor taste when they are sitting on some of the best fishing, crabbing and oyster grounds in the state? The community stores on all three islands do a brisk trade in tinned seafood, as do primitive traders from PNG who load their dugouts with live muddies each week to sell to Queensland Islanders for $2 each. It's a major source of income for the PNG traders who have to hunt and fish to survive.

You have to wonder if natural food-gathering skills are being lost on Queensland islands because it is more convenient to hunt and fish at the local store.

WEIPA

Fishing Made Easy

It was pretty disappointing when Bill Strike was almost forty-five minutes late picking us up for a fishing trip at Weipa. Hugh and I were sitting on the pub steps. There were only a couple of hours of daylight left and we had to be back at the hotel by dark. We were pretty disappointed also when we found out he still had to launch his boat, motor a good few kilometres upstream *and* catch the bait before we even wet a line, and here it was after five p.m.

But we didn't say anything because Bill's sort of built like the proverbial brick toilet block and he looks like he could fly off the handle if the mood took him. So we just thought, what the hell? Who wants to catch stupid fish anyway? It's usually a big yawn just feeding them for no result.

Worse still, up in the Gulf they have this infuriating little fish called the mud skipper that surfaces right in front of you and stares mockingly with its bug eyes. They mocked us unmercifully a week before down the Gulf at Karumba, coming out of the murky water to stare pop-eyed as we fished off the beach. Unfortunately they're as fast as they are dumb-looking because as hard as I tried to belt them over the head with the butt of my rod, the more they bobbed up to gloat.

But back at Weipa things didn't get any better when Bill finally picked us up and we got to the boat ramp to be told by a mate there was no bait around, and anyway it didn't matter because there were no fish being caught.

He'd been out all day and the only scale he'd seen was on the one that got away. Bill just smiled and took off at a million knots upstream, pointing out where he'd seen a big crocodile a week or two earlier.

This reminded him of a fishing trip he made last year up to old Bertiehaugh Station on the Ducie River with cattleman Rod Heinemann. They were fishing for barra when a small croc came floating down the river.

"Old Rod can call a croc in close by howling like a dingo," said Bill. "He started howling like a dog so we could get a better look and pretty soon up came this bloody big grandfather crocodile that had to be at least fifteen feet. It was a little bit more than we bargained for so we shut up after that."

Back at Weipa, with the sun sinking fast, Bill swung off the main stream into a tiny creek snaking through the mangroves, still doing a million knots. A mate told us later Bill likes speeding through the tiny creeks because it often frightens the living daylights out of sleeping crocodiles, sending them diving for the water only metres away from the boat. This in turn frightens the living daylights out of any unsuspecting visitors in the boat like Hugh and yours truly, which in turn gives Bill a great laugh.

We didn't happen to bump into any crocs that day and by this time it was about an hour away from sundown, and we still didn't even have bait. Right about then Bill throttled back to an idle, took a quick look along the shallow water, climbed nimbly up on to the bow and in the next couple of minutes had caught all the live mullet bait we needed for a day's fishing in just two expert casts with his bait net. There was a bonus too, because a half dozen small prawns came in with the net and Bill gobbled one down, urging us to try some. So we munched them down with reluctance; and they weren't half bad either, as raw prawns go.

But it was fishing, not gourmet meals, we were on about that sundown, so we rocketed back to the mouth of the small creek, thankful again that no crocodiles jumped into the boat. We anchored at the mouth where

Bill pointed out the ripples made by fish feeding close to the bank and landed his bait right in the centre. His line had hardly settled when it was hit by a three kilogram king salmon.

"They said there was no bait, hey?" he said triumphantly. "They said there were no fish, hey? They just don't know how to catch fish," he laughed. "It's all in the way you hold your mouth, see," and he pulled a cock-eyed, twisted face that had us all in fits.

Half an hour later we had five king salmon between three and four kilograms each and were back at the pub right on sundown. Just two-and-a-half hours after sitting on the pub steps moaning to each other about Bill being late, the three of us were sitting down to a great meal of king salmon.

"Pity it wasn't barramundi, but king salmon isn't a bad substitute," Bill said.

If you ever run into Bill Strike and he can't catch you a fish and make you laugh at the same time, then you could be six feet under and don't know it. But there's one thing to be careful about on first meeting a bush expert like Bill Strike. He's a great fishing and hunting mate of brewery boss Bernard Power and like a lot of people in the bush, he's particularly loyal to his mates.

So when Bill wants to shout and asks you what will it be, don't be like my mate Sawrey who said: Why thanks, Bill, I'll have a cold Fourex — because you won't get it. When Bill Strike shouts you, drink Power's or you don't drink at all. And once you set eyes on Bill Strike, expert hunter, fisherman and drinker, you won't feel inclined to argue the toss.

KARUMBA

Barramundi Jenny Nets a Croc

The cultured English accent of Jenny Lott hardly seemed appropriate coming from someone dressed in dusty, oil-stained T-shirt and shorts. Nor did her corded, sun-baked arms and strong hands, or what she was saying about her life as a lone Gulf of Carpentaria barramundi fisherwoman.

"It was low tide and the crocodile caught in my nets was very much alive and stranded well up the creek bank in the mud. I wanted to get going but I had to get the crocodile out before I could recover my nets.

"I don't carry firearms on board and we don't kill crocodiles anyway, so I grabbed a very large spanner from the boat, crawled through the mud until I was beside the crocodile and hit it over the head until it was rendered unconscious. Then I untangled the net, left the crocodile to recover, and headed for home."

No, this articulate English woman was not reading the script for *Crocodile Dundee III*, but relating an experience from her thirty years of prawn trawling, mackerel and barra fishing from Townsville through Torres Strait and the Gulf right up to the Northern Territory border.

For the last ten years she has settled for the lonely life of barra fishing by herself, sometimes working up to several hundred kilometres out of her Karumba base for as long as eight weeks. The trips can vary from three to eight weeks, just as long as it takes the former air hostess to fill her boat's deep freeze with one tonne of barramundi fillets.

Like most of the free spirits I have met over the years she tends to play down the dangers of her trade but old barra fishermen around the Gulf town say it's no job for the foolish or faint-hearted. They mainly fish the isolated estuaries, living on board their barra boats and setting and clearing their nets from small tin dinghies that can run the shallow muddy waters of Gulf rivers and creeks. Whole families live on board the bigger barra boats, the children studying at sea by correspondence.

Besides the obvious dangers of crocodiles and sharks there are the stingers, deadly box jellyfish, which habitually get caught in the nets. Stingers are one of the great fears of barra fishermen. Quite often their deadly shreds are sprayed around by big barra thrashing wildly as the nets are hauled in.

"I've always had a fear of copping a piece of the stinger in the eyes when I'm up some little creek, maybe miles away from the big boat," one barra man told me. "You'd be dead before you could call help."

Jenny Lott agrees there are risks but says it's all a matter of taking care, applying common sense and maintaining your gear in top condition. "You don't jump into the water, and the crocodiles and sharks won't jump into your boat. It's a pretty good arrangement,"

I first heard of Jenny Lott many years ago in most unusual circumstances. I was off Mooloolaba with former surf champion Kim McKenzie, who had the government shark meshing contract for the Sunshine Coast at the time. It was an eerie scene as chief photographer Jim Fenwick and I watched Kim go about her business, which included hanging upside down over the gunwale of her Sharkcat to disembowel and examine the stomach contents of meshed sharks.

As she hung there, hacking away at the underbelly above a seemingly bottomless clear blue ocean, the dead shark's mate suddenly appeared a metre or two below. It was a tiger shark about three and a half metres long and it just glided gracefully below this strange scene, which was giving Fenwick and me the shivers.

When Kim finished the task and was once again up-right on deck, I mentioned that her job was a lot more dangerous than I had imagined. She seemed mildly surprised.

"If you think this job is dangerous you should talk to an English woman I met up north recently. She's a barra fisherwoman and she's out for weeks on her own with the crocs and sharks. You wouldn't catch me doing that."

It took me a few years to catch up with Jenny Lott but the wait was worth it. The daughter of a Royal Air Force officer, Jenny was born under a wandering star and travelled around with her parents from postings at one RAF base to the next. She worked as an air hostess wth a charter company, British Eagle, and became interested in Australia through Aussie workmates.

About thirty years ago she and a couple of mates bought an old car and drove as far as they could in the direction of Australia. She eventually landed in Perth and worked as a house mistress in a girls school. A year later she had saved enough to travel to Queensland and was in Townsville when her money ran out.

"While I was in Townsville I had the chance to go out on a trawler, caught plenty of fish, saw the Barrier Reef for the first time and fell in love with the place. I needed money so I took a job on a trawler."

That was the start of her fishing career, a career that has taken her into some of the most dangerous waters and wildest, most remote country in Australia. She flies back to see her family in England every two years and once again experience some of the refinements of her youth.

"It's a good feeling to be able to shower when you want to and not be covered in engine oil or mud all the time," she said.

What do her English friends and family think of her life in the wilds of Australia?

"They don't understand the environment out here. They have no concept of what it's like."

As a matter of fact it is hard for an Aussie to come to

terms with a cultured English woman crawling through the mud of some remote Gulf river to belt a three metre crocodile over the head.

But at fifty-three, how long can someone continue a life like that? "As long as I can. It will be a few years yet, I hope," said Jenny.

After that she'll move across Cape York Peninsula to Mossman where she has a few acres of land in the rainforest.

"I'd miss the fishing but it's a beautiful place at Mossman and I have a horse back there. We had horses when I was growing up in England and I still love them."

But the horses will have to wait because right now Jenny is too busy fishing the Gulf streams and no doubt hoping she doesn't have to render any more crocodiles unconscious with a very large spanner.

KARUMBA

Laika Orbits In

The next time I heard from Jenny Lott she was coming to terms with the loss of her only companion on those long barra fishing trips into the Gulf, her little dog Semper. Semper spent much of her life on board Jenny's boat, was not used to mainland traffic and was run over by a car in Karumba.

Maybe it was part of the healing process; Jenny wrote a beautiful tribute to Semper and sent it to me. It was published in the *Courier-Mail*. Not surprisingly loneliness was the topic of conversation when I spoke to her about the story shortly before she cast off from Karumba on her next fishing trip.

That little dog meant a great deal to Jenny, you could tell from her story, but help was on the way because she had been promised a tiny pup, a full sister to Semper, just as soon as it was old enough to leave its mother.

As I said, few women would have as lonely a job as this British air hostess turned fisherwoman. During the nine-month barra season she is at sea for as long as it takes to fill her one-tonne freezer with fillets — anything up to two months. She then heads in to Karumba with the catch and is out fishing again as soon as possible.

Sound pretty lonely? To you and me, maybe, but to those on the horizons of Queensland it is more human company than enough. As we talked I mused about the seemingly lonely people I have met throughout the state and compared Jenny's job with the life of a monumental loner I met in the pub at Hungerford.

Max Dean and his grader keep the dingo fence clear of desert sand and scrub between Hungerford and Cameron Corner, in Queensland's extreme southwest. He is on the track eleven months of the year. I was telling Jenny how Max told me, quite seriously, of the parties he sometimes has in the middle of the desert.

"We don't have 'em all the time, you know," Max said, "but every so often you strike travellers going down one track or another and when you bump into someone out there, well, it's only polite to offer them a drink; and you know how it is, you have one or two drinks and the next thing it's a party."

I always get a laugh from that one — the mental picture of Max and a travelling drover or fencer sitting down in the middle of the desert for a party. The Nobby's Nuts people could do something with that. But Jenny wasn't laughing because she understood what Max was on about.

"Yes," she said thoughtfully. "It's a bit like that out in the Gulf. You don't see many other fishermen because we steer clear of each other when we're working. We don't crowd each other. But occasionally a passing boat might come in to shelter overnight and it's just like that grader driver says. Suddenly you're cooking up a barbecue and it's amazing where you can find a beer when you want one, even in the middle of the Gulf."

They may be at opposite ends of Queensland, one in the desert and one on the ocean, but they are kindred spirits in isolation on the edge of civilisation, Max and Jenny.

It's quite amazing also how isolated individuals like Jenny keep in touch with the outside world. I wrote to her last month requesting the urgent return of a *Courier-Mail* photograph of herself and Semper to go with her essay on Semper's death. It was the only one in existence. I enclosed a large self-addressed envelope.

She was fishing in Van Diemen's Inlet, about seventy kilometres north of Karumba, when a fisherman cruised in and handed her my package. The fishing was slow and she was weeks away from returning to Karumba and, as she said later, there is a great lack of letter boxes around Van Diemen's Inlet.

In fact there is nothing at Van Diemen's Inlet except mangroves, mud flats, mozzies, sand flies and saltpans. But there was a professional crabber working in the mangroves who sometimes sent live muddies to southern markets by light plane via Cairns.

Surprisingly, light planes have no trouble landing on Gulf saltpans during the Dry. Over the years barra fishermen like Jenny have erected wind socks on saltpans near many of the isolated Gulf rivers and creeks to aid landing when they urgently need to get fish out or spare parts in. We were in luck. A light plane was due within days and we got the photo, via fishing boat, dinghy, shanks's pony through the mud and across mangroves and saltpans, light plane and jet.

In the next week or two Jenny will take her dinghy into the mangroves at Van Diemen's Inlet again, plough through the mud and across the saltpan to collect another package from another light plane. The package will not contain a photo of a dog but the real thing, a five-week-old full sister to Semper. It could be a twin sister it is so like Semper, according to Jenny. It was too young to take from the mother when she saw it but she arranged for a light plane on a regular run to Gulf cattle stations to land on Van Diemen's Inlet saltpan and hand it over.

Appropriately for a dog that will fly in from space, it has been named Laika, after the Soviet dog that became the first earthling in space aboard Sputnik II in 1957. One morning very soon Jenny Lott will not be alone on her boat in some distant, isolated Gulf stream making a living catching barramundi.

CLONCURRY

A Long Way from Home

Understandable misconceptions about Cape York Peninsula as a tropical paradise disappear with each dusty bend on the bumpy 800 kilometre drive from Cooktown to the Tip. While parts of the eastern coastline are pristine South Sea havens, the road up Queensland's spine spears endlessly through ordinary Australian bush. The coasts are out of sight and tropical growth on the road is sparse until you reach the Tip.

Instead of passing the long driving hours imagining yourself under swaying palms by a blue lagoon, you find yourself marvelling at the explorers and the pioneering cattlemen, and the prospectors who followed hot on their heels, almost 150 years ago. You ask yourself: How did they cover those vast distances on foot, even on horseback? How did they survive distance, snakes, crocodiles and constant battle with Aborigines?

Not surprisingly, many explorers did not return and probably the most tragic were those in Edmund Kennedy's disastrous 1848 expedition from Rockingham Bay (Cardwell) to Cape York. Out of thirteen in the party, ten died or were killed by Aborigines, including Kennedy. Ironically, it was an Aborigine, Jacky Jacky, who was the hero of the expedition, making a final solo dash against all odds to Cape York in a vain attempt to get help.

Okay, we've all heard of Jacky Jacky's epic dash, but you don't appreciate the hurdles and dangers until you've travelled the land. It's rugged going, even in the open country, but hitting the rainforests is like hitting a giant wall of green-black concrete. The jungle closes in on the narrow tracks and it's hard to imagine a kangaroo rat squeezing through, let alone a man. Kennedy's party was shocked by the density of the jungles of the extreme north — they had expected "wooded hills", as reported by sailors looking through spyglasses from passing ships.

You learn to appreciate Jacky Jacky's grit and skill when you've seen the country. Sixteen years later, brothers Frank and Alick Jardine, hardly out of their teens, followed in Kennedy's wake to the tip without loss of life, blazing a track that signalled the coming of the pioneers. Meanwhile in 1861, the ill-fated explorers Burke and Wills had crossed Australia from south to north, ending on Flinders River not far from where Karumba stands on the Gulf of Carpentaria. They perished on the return journey, due mainly to Burke's stubborn streak which was blamed for everything that went wrong with the expedition.

In an age when any link with history can earn tourist dollars, it is not surprising that many Gulf Country locals like to claim Burke and Wills passed their way. Down in Cloncurry they know they did, because Burke named their river the Cloncurry after a spot back in his native Ireland. Six years after Burke and Wills passed into history, a pastoralist explorer, Ernest Henry, arrived on the Cloncurry River looking for grazing land but turned to prospecting and eventually found substantial copper deposits. The discovery led to one of the strangest, shortest and least known migration stories in Australia's history.

Poor Henry had much more enthusiasm than money to get his El Dorado up and running, and the fact that the nearest Gulf port was Normanton, 400 kilometres away through virgin bush, did not excite would-be investors. Gold fever was sweeping Australia and investors were not interested in a copper mine out where the crows flew backwards, so Henry sailed to England in 1867 hoping to raise money. Unfortunately, it was the same story over there. Not only were they not interested in Cloncurry copper, they didn't even know where on God's earth Queensland was, let alone Cloncurry.

Failing to get financial backing, Henry did the strangest thing. He hired thirty Cornish miners and put them on a ship to Australia. Why he went to this expense is a mystery. It could have been for their mining experience but he should have known experience was nowhere near as important in this project as an ability to live and work in hell, which is how the Cornishmen described their conditions later. But they had no way of knowing that when they landed at Normanton, a major port of entry in those days.

Today, Normanton residents like to tell you of the number of visitors who claim their ancestors first set foot on Aussie soil at Normanton, and if you have been there lately you will probably say nothing much has changed. Normanton is living history. I don't imagine it would have made much of an impression on the Cornishmen, but much worse was to come. Almost immediately they were loaded on to bullock drays and driven 400 kilometres through trackless bush in the summer heat and flies. An eternity later they arrived at the mine site to find they would be housed in bough sheds, and live on salt beef, damper and muddy water. They stayed in the 45°C heat long enough to dig one drayload of copper ore, then downed tools and demanded to be taken back to Normanton and shipped home. You wonder what tales they told of their Cloncurry trip back in Cornwall and how the stories would have been embellished. Still, generations of northerners have survived those hardships and today, in some cases, circumstances are not greatly changed. So it isn't surprising to find that Henry's copper mine succeeded without Cornish expertise, and Cloncurry was born.

Conned by a Thick Hide

Normanton, at the bottom right-hand corner of the Gulf of Carpentaria, doesn't often make the news. Oh, sure, it gets a flurry of media attention every couple of decades when a cyclone devastates the north, but apart from that it never rates a mention on merit alone and not without reason. Observant visitors will soon discover this business heart of the vast Gulf cattle country isn't exactly bustling.

One night I walked along the main thoroughfare from my hotel, the Purple Pub, past a marvellous shanty pub, the Central, and on to the Albion Hotel, another great shanty. After a round or two with some cattlemen, a happy layabout, and some pig dogs with six-inch-wide leather collars, I returned to my pub and went to slumberland lulled by Slim Dusty who croons around the clock at the Purple Pub.

Next day about noon I returned to the main street and saw my footprints clear and untrampled in the fine red dust despite sixteen hours of foot traffic along the town's busiest footpath. Maybe it will take another cyclone to erase such flimsy evidence of a wanderer's presence in a town where daily life hardly seems to stir the dust. Workaday wheels turn real slow in Normanton.

About the most exciting thing to happen there for a long time was the recently introduced Community Development Employment Program. At least, everyone mentions it. Under this scheme people who want to can do community work for the dole and it works pretty well because Normanton may be old and dusty but it's very clean. The drawback is that volunteers get paid weekly instead of the dole fortnightly which leads to payday booze-up problems once a week instead of once a fortnight.

What can you do besides drink to escape the slow life of Normanton? You can catch the Gulflander, the train plying between Normanton and Croydon, an old gold-mining town that collapsed when gold finally ran out in 1920. If you don't like it there you can catch the train right back, because that's the extent of the century-old, 152-kilometre Queensland government rail line in the middle of nowhere that hasn't made a profit since 1907. But it is a ride you should not miss.

Back in Normanton you would be mad to ignore the old buildings. Many have gone but one stands tall and proud as the headquarters of the Carpentaria Shire Council. Others like the Purple Pub don't look so good outside, but if you can make it through the crowded public bar where a lot of locals spend a lot of time, there is a quiet bar and dining room out the back.

I was dining there recently, between making tracks on the main street, looking at the wall and wondering what I could write to the folks back home on a postcard from Normanton. I didn't mind the stuffed two metre crocodile staring angrily down from the wall or the dusty boomerangs and buffalo horns, but the bullock hide hanging by my table brought back unpleasant memories of far-off Brisbane.

Back there in the Breakfast Creek Hotel a couple of years ago a bloke I didn't know stepped up, handed me a dirty big brown paper bundle and said: "Gidday mate. That's the first of 'em. That'll be fifty bucks."

The first of what? What fifty dollars?

"The first of the bullock hides you ordered right here in the public bar last night, and I'll have the other three next week. Don't you remember?"

Of course I didn't remember but I wasn't going to reveal

myself as the memory-shot welsher I really am. So I borrowed fifty bucks, told him I wasn't going to plait a mile-long greenhide rope after all and cancelled the other hides. Your home may be different, but mine is not the place to take the hide off Strawberry's back, particularly late at night. If you've seen what happens to Dagwood Bumstead when he gets home with the stuffed moose head he didn't mean to buy at the auction because he sneezed at the wrong time, then you've got a fair idea what happened to me and my cowhide that night.

It went into the boot of my car for the next couple of weeks until I got this wonderful idea about how I could off-load the hide and make myself out to be a swell fellow indeed. I unloaded it free and unencumbered to the Valleys Rugby League Club ladies committee to raffle, because the club was going through hard times back then. Even so it took some fast talking before they finally accepted it and made a couple of hundred bucks on the deal.

Back in the Purple Pub's dining room I began to wonder if this same bloke didn't come through Normanton a few years ago, look around the bar for a goose like me and say: "Gidday mate. Here's your bullock hide. I'll have the other thirty tomorrow. That'll be fifty bucks." He's probably got a semi-trailer load outside, travelling around Queensland in ever-diminishing circles looking for suckers like me.

So think twice before you buy your next bullock hide. And if you ever come to Normanton expect to make a deep impression, at least on the main street.

SAWREY
'91

MT GARNET

The Man from Mt Fullstop

Distance has never been a problem for Australians heading for the races. Long before the motor car, let alone the aeroplane, racegoers were riding horses, walking, or driving spring carts long distances to the annual picnic meet.

Things haven't changed much. Last year I was leaning against the Birdsville Hotel drinking a beer and feeling pretty smart, along with a couple of thousand other happy people, when a dusty motorcyclist rode into town, staggered off his bike, lay down in the main street and went to sleep. He'd just ridden more than 3000 kilometres from Perth. The day before, some other blokes drove an ancient tractor up the Birdsville Track from Adelaide.

Of course, the Birdsville meet is not your average Aussie picnic outing but, for me at least, it characterises the Aussie bush races, however overstated, where the bush meets the city for just a fleeting few hours a year. I'd say my old man, and his old man, got their first look at a fair dinkum city joker at a country race meeting somewhere in central Queensland. That type of culture shock continues today, not that it is always a shock for the bushies.

Sawrey and I had a bit of a surprise when we stumbled into Mt Garnet races on our trip up Cape York Peninsula. Driving up the back roads from Townsville, I imagined this three-day race and rodeo meet would be like all the others, with tents and caravans scattered around like ragged hordes of gypsies. It came as a surprise to find that the Mt Garnet races are a very structured affair with a social pecking order established over many, many years by the district's pioneering families. This social order extends to permanent private camps in prime positions next to the racetrack. The camps range from huge, open-ended dining rooms, kitchens and bars, with showers and toilets, and catering for scores of family and friends, to similar amenities in more modest lean-tos in lesser positions.

If you are in the know, as Hugh and I somehow managed to be, you will find yourself invited to unroll your swag at one of these favoured sites. If you are not, then you can take your chances in the public camping ground with the great unwashed and fight for a feed and a beer at the public stalls, which was tough luck for the rest of the mob. As it turned out, Hugh and I received favoured sleeping quarters under a tank stand, right next door to our host's private shower — five-star bush accommodation really. We were high on the pecking order at the Mt Garnet races and happy to be so after a couple of nights camped in the scrub.

It is not hard to see why the pioneering families of the district have established comfortable quarters, even at play, just once a year. Their ancestors did it tough long before they arrived in the northern wilderness in the middle of last century and, no doubt, the desire to improve their lot is instilled in the sons and daughters of the pioneers from their earliest years.

The story of just one Mt Garnet pioneering family, the Atkinsons, is an endurance epic of Hollywood proportions. Back in 1863, when the north was largely unexplored, James Atkinson, his wife, and baby daughter travelled overland by horse and wagon, pushing a mob of sheep from Port Fairy in southern Victoria, a distance of about 2500 kilometres. The journey across the trackless continent took two and a half years, during which time a son was born. Today, the Atkinson clan is spread across the state but is still a major influence in the Mt Garnet district — and nowhere more so than at the races.

It was in the Atkinson camp, over a friendly glass or two, that we discovered that the once-famed bush wit has not been dulled by television and video which floods the outback today. There we met the boss of Mt Fullstop Station, Mac Core.

Mac has been many things in the bush over the years, from grazier to racehorse owner to industry organiser. But he may be best remembered for a remarkable poem, a parody of what really happened to every Aussie's hero, The Man from Snowy River. Mac and some friends wrote the poem and even the Banjo would have roared approval to hear Mac Core recite it in animated reverie.

You all thought "The Man" gave a cheer as he raced his hardy pony down the mountain like a torrent down its bed, eh? Wrong! The nag was too stupid to stop and plunged over the top with The Man's terrified screams sounding like cheers of bravado to his spellbound mates above.

You thought he chased Old Regret's mob until they halted, cowed and beaten, right? Nah! The Man and his stupid nag were lost and going in circles when the mob, blocked by a blind gully, came trotting back. The Man and his pony simply tagged along — "and alone and unassisted brought them back". Well that's the way the man from Mt Fullstop called it, anyway.

Meanwhile, around the Mt Garnet racetrack, a few glazed-eyed, open-mouthed young bumpkins were heavily engaged in their annual cultural exchange with a city slicker with an easy smile and a white stetson. He was showing them how to make a quid by tossing two pennies in the air and they kept paying him for the education. Where would our culture be without a country race meeting education?